Kingdom Come

Understanding
the Book of Revelation

Ed Townley

Kingdom Come

Understanding
the Book of Revelation

Ed Townley

Unity Village, Missouri

Kingdom Come
A Unity Books Paperback Original

Unity Books are available at special discounts for bulk purchases for study groups, book clubs, sales promotions, book signings or fundraising. To place an order, call the Unity Customer Care Department at 1-866-236-3571 or email *wholesaleaccts@unityonline.org*.

Bible quotations are from the New Revised Standard Version unless otherwise noted.

Cover design: Tom Truman
Interior design: The Covington Group, Kansas City, Missouri

Library of Congress Control Number: 2012947695

ISBN: 978-0-87159-361-0

Canada BN 13252 0933 RT

This book is dedicated, with love and deep appreciation, to the congregations of Unity in Chicago and Unity of Dallas, who not only endured but warmly supported my Revelation fascination; and to Unity of Greater Hartford, the wonderful spiritual community that challenged me to finally get it all down on paper.

CONTENTS

INTRODUCTION

L ooking back, I think it started for me in the cave. It's not a physically impressive cave, as these things go. Still, the fact that I was there at all was so astonishing, and the energies of the place so strong, that the memory remains vivid even now, a dozen years later.

The cave is on Patmos, a small Greek island near the coast of Turkey in the Aegean Sea. It is the place where, in the late first century of the Common Era, a religious exile named John wrote his descriptions of a detailed and specific personal spiritual vision. His language was so vivid, and his imagery so intense, that his writing has haunted Christians and actually affected the course of history for more than 2,000 years.

It was my first trip to Greece—well, my first trip anywhere, really. At the time I was senior minister at Unity in Chicago, a lively spiritual community, part of the worldwide Unity movement and decidedly on what would be considered the liberal end of the Christianity spectrum. I had been asked to serve as a kind of spiritual tour guide for a small group on a two-week exploration of Greece and the Aegean islands.

By the time we arrived on Patmos, I was already in a profound spiritual fog—to the point that my traveling companions had become concerned. I had long felt "called" to Greece, more strongly than to any other place on the planet. I expected to find natural beauty, impressive ruins and a deep sense of time and history—and it was all there. What I hadn't expected was an all-pervasive spiritual energy so intense and alive that it left me reeling and nearly delirious. In fact, I spent two days in bed, not really sick but with a high fever and vivid dreams of Furies and flies. (I think perhaps the flies were a result of having recently reread Sartre's play about Orestes pursued by vengeful flies.)

I had expected to be visiting the ruins of a long-dead, pantheistic religious tradition. What I found instead was a profound sense of immediate, eternal Spirit, very much alive, and very eager to embrace me in its power and purpose. I quickly came to realize that this was not a distinct and specific energy; it was a particular expression of the One—the only energy there is. I understood that it is relatively unimportant whether we talk of many gods and goddesses with distinctive personalities or many distinct aspects of One Presence, One Power. The truth is the same. The infinite Love that is God eagerly assumes whatever characters or qualities we may need as we struggle to reclaim our own Oneness—our absolute unity with the divine.

Out of my feverish delirium and chaotic awareness, I wrote a poem. It's the one piece of my own writing that I continue to reread and refer back to as I move forward on my own path.

Now, except for high school writing assignments, I had not written poetry before; and I have not felt called to write any more poetry in the ensuing years. But it seemed to be the only way I could process my thoughts and emotions in that particular moment. This is what I wrote:

Aegean Fever

Here's what I know!
(Come close so I can whisper;
It's all too new to speak aloud to skeptics;
Although that day, I know, is coming soon.)

Here's what I know:
The ancient gods and goddesses are back!

Their temples here are throbbing now with passion,
Not empty echoes of a dusty, distant past.

The ancient gods and goddesses are back!
They move and work among us,
No longer distanced in Olympian mystic heights.
They call us to them, they awaken deep within us
Forgotten powers to create a sacred world.

The ancient gods and goddesses are back!
We thought them dead,
We thought that they'd been vanquished
By greater powers of newer, jealous gods.
We thought that we had outgrown ancient stories,
Too simple to affect our complex lives.

Still they return, and still their powers move us,
And still we need to feel their tireless love.

The ancient gods and goddesses are back!
But they have never really been away.
They have been waiting deep within us;
And our lives are now exploded
By the power of their laughter, and their love.

The ancient gods and goddesses are back!
O happy fate! To welcome them within me
And to feel their powers surging through me now.

So this is who and how I was as I stood in that cave on Patmos.
I had come to sense the Aegean as a vast, spiritual whirlpool in
which many different religious traditions—Hellenistic, Jewish,
Christian, Muslim and others unnamed—had clashed and combined, blended and separated from prehistoric times to the
present—and beyond.

That morning, on a whim, I had tucked my small travel Bible in among my water bottle, sunblock, seasick pills and other necessities of the day. As we stood together in the timeless cave, and more out of a sense of ministerial duty than from any clear spiritual guidance, I began to read aloud to my fellow travelers the opening words of the Revelation to John:

> The revelation of Jesus Christ, which God gave him to show his servants what must soon take place; he made it known by sending his angel to his servant John, who testified to the word of God and to the testimony of Jesus Christ, even to all that he saw. Blessed is the one who reads aloud the words of the prophecy, and blessed are those who hear and who keep what is written in it; for the time is near.
>
> —Rev. 1:1-3

The moment truly felt eternal. When I looked up, other visitors to the cave had quietly gathered around. I read a few more verses and stopped. There was a deep silence, filled with infinite energy. I have rarely felt more aware of the spiritual quality of Oneness: Not just the Oneness of all of us gathered in the cave, and not just Oneness with the mysterious author who had written those words so long ago. That was all there, of course. But around and within and beyond all of that, I felt a Oneness with eternal Spirit, and with all the ways in which that Spirit has been approached, and has expressed, as our collective human journey unfolds.

That cave experience remains a treasured memory—difficult to explain, impossible to forget. Not long afterward, the first in the *Left Behind* series of books appeared, and became an immediate best-seller, not only among religious titles but on general fiction lists as well. Curious as always, I read the first book—and felt an immediate sense of revulsion. The Revelation to

John, around which I had felt such an energy of spiritual power that was both intensely personal and absolutely universal, was presented as a work of anger, judgment, conflict and chaos. The message was the antithesis of universal; it insisted that only those who embraced and obeyed normative Christianity (as defined, of course, by the authors) had any hope of survival or spiritual reward. All others were doomed to various punishments, described in excruciating detail, and to eternal damnation without even the slightest hope of a second chance.

At this time I had not allowed that cave experience to lead me further into the Revelation itself. But I had begun to find great joy—and positive reinforcement—in the pages and stories of the rest of the Bible. I had learned to approach it with fresh eyes—to approach it, in fact, *maieutically*. This intimidating-sounding word comes from the Greek for "midwife." It suggests that the role of any teacher or minister is not to tell students what they need to believe, but to help them give birth to the knowing that they already hold in deepest consciousness. The teacher is thus a midwife, and every student is already pregnant—and has fully come to term—with spiritual truth.

Using this maieutic method, and understanding the Bible as a kind of personal travel guide describing the spiritual Hero's Journey from the Adam consciousness of Genesis to the Christ Consciousness of the teachings of Jesus, I was able to find clarity, comfort and practical support in every book of both Hebrew Scripture and the Christian New Testament.

Well, almost every book. I still steered clear of the Revelation. Even before the *Left Behind* series, I was certainly aware that many people found in the Bible's final book a lot of justification for beliefs that I did not share—belief in a God of judgment and eternal punishment, belief in a dualistic world of constant danger, conflict and warfare, belief that our spiritual presence in human form was the ultimate divine punishment for a long-ago sin of hubris that God simply could not, or would not, forgive.

I may not have shared these beliefs, but—as I've come to realize—that doesn't mean they don't affect me. My relatively newborn faith in our individual and unique Oneness with the divine, and the spiritually important creative purpose that brings us into human expression, was still a little tentative. I didn't want to risk exposing my beliefs to the negative energy I believed to be lurking in the images of Revelation. I held my Patmos memories dear, and I didn't want to risk losing them in a book of darkness and gloom.

I've come to realize that many of us feel that way. No longer able or willing to accept dualistic religious beliefs, we're still afraid that their collective power might overwhelm the love-based energy that is working in our lives. Some avoid the entire Bible out of an unfounded fear that it might contradict our new faith. Many more pick and choose selectively. The Gospels are fine, of course, and Genesis is okay as spiritually guided folklore. Some of the Psalms are helpful, as is Paul on a good day. But very, very few think of Revelation as anything but a dark and angry contradiction of everything we have come to believe.

I didn't read any more of the *Left Behind* books. But as time went on, questions arose, articles appeared, and assumptions I considered to be contrary to both faith and logic seemed to be taking hold in our shared consciousness. I finally decided that if the Bible was to be my chosen road map to the kingdom, I had to be comfortable with all of it. I needed to march fearlessly through the Revelation to John, trusting that the love and empowerment of the Gospels could also be found in this final book of the Bible.

This book is the result of that process. Far from a grudging acceptance of the Revelation, I have come to enthusiastically appreciate the realistic and loving way in which it describes the Hero's Journey that each of us is called to experience—again and again!—as we set about accomplishing the spiritual work that is our whole purpose for coming into the limitations of mortality.

Finding a way to share that enthusiasm has been a real challenge. That's why you may find that this book has something of a split personality. (Not that there's anything wrong with that!) On the one hand, it is a record of one man's personal process of wrestling with the Revelation, and the understanding it offers on some of the challenges and turning points of my own life. On the other hand, I've created a more impersonal analysis—chapter by chapter, sometimes verse by verse—of the Revelation from a perspective that is appreciative, spiritual and metaphysical, but not directly related to the dogma or history of any particular church.

It didn't start out to be so schizophrenic. My original focus was limited to the text itself and to understanding it from a fresh perspective. But I've come to believe that only by including both elements—the personal and the interpretive—can I hope to achieve the larger goal that became clear as my work continued. That goal is to appreciate the Revelation, not as an apocalyptic vision of the end of the world, but as a practical, personal guide to the spiritual process—what Joseph Campbell called the Hero's Journey—that each of us is engaged in, knowingly or not, every moment of our lives.

What I know best about that journey is, of course, how it has expressed in my own life in astonishing ways—and I've centered my ministry in my willingness to share that story with others. I have made many mistakes, lost many battles, stumbled accidentally into astonishing victories, and slowly begun to understand and express a dimension of awareness and personal empowerment that allows me—sometimes—to move more efficiently through the interplay of shadows and light that this human experience involves and requires.

The Book of Revelation has been, for me, a useful tool for the fine detail work this process demands. It is more willing than any "self-help" book to acknowledge the tremendous power that appearances of duality can exert in our human lives. I hope some of my own adventures may encourage others to open their hearts and minds to its reassuring message.

The Revelation to John also helps me stay awake to the "bigger picture" when I tend to get lost in my own small dramas. Like all true Scripture, it offers clarity and practical support as I encounter the unique challenges and choices of the day. It also encourages me to keep going by evoking the new dimension of spiritual consciousness that expresses through me, and that becomes the shared new dimension of the human experience that Jesus Christ named the "kingdom of heaven."

As we can clearly read throughout the New Testament—in the Gospels, the Revelation to John and the assorted letters of Paul and others—this kingdom is not meant to be thought of as a spiritual possibility limited to the afterlife. It is rather a new consciousness in which we can—and will—live out the balance of our human experiences.

Achieving this kingdom consciousness is the entire purpose for which we eternal spiritual beings have come into this mortal illusion of duality and limitation. It begins with a spark of faith, and it requires us to move forward through distractions, illusions, fears and false beliefs with our focus firmly fixed on our purpose and goal. Step by careful step, we are guided to the depths of negative expression—not as a threat, not as a judgment, but as an assurance that no matter how dark things get, the outcome is well worth the journey.

Using the Revelation to John as an instrument of spiritual support, however, cannot ignore the fact that this dramatic and apocalyptic book has been seen and used as something quite different throughout the two millennia since it was written. To many passionate Christians, the Revelation is not about a loving spiritual energy eager to express through us as a new dimension of the process of Creation. To them it is rather a highly dualistic view of life as a constant battle between the forces of a resentful and judgmental God and those of a cruel, jealous and vindictive Beast eager to lure us into an eternal abyss of darkness and pain—with each of us trapped somewhere in the spectrum between God and the Beast.

For these people who either wield the Revelation as a weapon of attack or avoid it as a relic of old, vengeful thinking, no personal stories will, by themselves, reconcile them to a new and positive view of an uncomfortable book. They already "know" what Revelation is all about; and they already "know" whether they accept it as a harsh and judgmental tool, or reject it as a crock.

It is to these people that I offer the second of the two paths that are interwoven throughout this book. To dissolve their fear-based convictions that nasty things lurk in the shadows of the Revelation, ready to devour any light-seeking soul who might venture in, the only effective approach is to move through its 22 chapters, verse by verse, until we're sure we can trust it, that no surprise attack is waiting around its next corner.

I do not claim to be a Bible scholar; I am at best a Bible *enthusiast*. Nor do I pretend to be an expert in how your spiritual path is—or should be—unfolding. It's all I can do to stay centered on my own path at any given moment.

What I do know is that the Revelation to John has a tremendous amount of clarity and loving support to offer when we approach it with a willingness to explore its metaphysical depths. To stay stubbornly stuck to its dramatic surface, fascinated by its imagery, steeped in duality, judgment, vengeance and eternal damnation, is a tragic mistake. To avoid it altogether out of fear of those same negative energies is equally misguided. We must go deeper. Our brains have an important role to play in understanding its imagery. But its true spiritual meaning, its loving outpicturing of our own Hero's Journeys, requires that we take it to our hearts. A heart-centered appreciation is the hope and intent of this book.

Understanding any spiritual writing requires that we first know something about when it was written, and by whom, and why. Of course, in its metaphysical depths, any spiritual writing is timeless—as relevant today as on the day it was written. But we can only reach that metaphysical perspective by recognizing and moving beneath the details of language, imagery and reference that anchor it in its time and place. So let's review what we know about the Revelation to John before we plunge into its murky depths.

About the Work

The Revelation to John is, without a doubt, the most controversial and contentious book of the Bible. On one hand are those who love it, quote it, use it to justify a whole range of opinions and prejudice, and wait eagerly for the day when the angry, judgmental and apocalyptic energy they find in the book comes to pass here on earth. (It's interesting to note that those who love the Revelation unanimously agree that its lurid pains and punishments will be inflicted on other people, not on them.) On the other hand are those who see in the Revelation's vivid imagery and judgmental attitude proof positive that the entire Bible is an antiquated remnant of religious superstition to be dismissed out of hand by anyone with a spiritual sensitivity.

As is usually the case in such religious battles, facts are the first victim. True, there aren't many facts about the Revelation to John we can affirm with absolute conviction. We're pretty sure where it was written but not when. And there's no certainty about whom the "John" who wrote it was. Still, it can't hurt to begin with a focus on what we do, in fact, know about the work—and what we don't.

As previously noted, we're told in the opening verse that the Revelation was written on the island of Patmos, off the coast of Asia Minor, by someone named John who had been banished to the island because of his insistence on preaching his Christian faith. (The faith of those who followed the teachings of Jesus Christ was not actually called "Christian" at the time, but it will help keep things simple if you'll allow me to use the term.)

There are almost as many men named John in the New Testament as there are women named Mary—and lacking any family names, nicknames or other clues, it's difficult to sort them out. There is a long-held tradition that says John, the "beloved disciple" who stood below the cross and to whom Jesus gave charge of his mother, was the same John who wrote five books of the New Testament—the fourth Gospel, the three epistles ascribed to "John" and the Revelation.

On the island of Patmos today, as well as among believers both in Greece and Turkey, it is firmly held that the disciple John brought Jesus' mother Mary north after the crucifixion, settling in a small house near Ephesus that can still be visited today. It was from there that he continued the apostolic work that resulted in his banishment to Patmos and the visionary experiences described in the Revelation.

It's a nice story; and indeed I found the spiritual energy around the cottage known as Mary's House to be incredibly powerful and deeply moving. But biblical scholars have pretty much agreed today that it can't be entirely true. The various writings are quite different stylistically, expressive of very different levels of literacy and education. Their perspectives on the message and meaning of Jesus Christ are equally varied.

Further, for the same person to have written them all, he would have had to be alive, healthy and extremely active for a very long time, particularly in terms of life spans at the time.

This leads to the question of when the Revelation was written. Again, there is no unanimity of opinion but a general consensus. Internal evidence and early church tradition set its composition at around the year 95 of the Common Era (A.D. in familiar reference). At that time, near the end of his reign, the Emperor Domitian had declared himself a god and required all subjects of the empire to publicly worship him as such. Since this is something early Christians could not or would not do, they were severely persecuted in large numbers—imprisoned, tortured and put to death. It was during this time of religious turmoil, some scholars believe, that John of Patmos, exiled from Asia Minor because of his faith, composed his Revelation as an affirmation to believers everywhere that beyond their present suffering lay the absolute assurance of victory and joy.

Other authorities argue for an earlier date of composition—perhaps 68 or 69 C.E., during the reign of Nero. Certainly the work was known by the middle of the second century, since there are references to it in other writings of that time. The earliest actual manuscript of the Revelation still in existence dates from the late second century.

More recent—and quite persuasive—scholarship suggests the author of the Revelation was not in exile from Rome at all, but rather from other Christians! He would have found in Asia Minor at the time Christian communities that coexisted comfortably in the shadows of major Roman temples and prevailing Roman customs. Tracing their spiritual roots largely to the Gentiles brought to the teachings of Jesus by the apostle Paul, they had little interest in the more conservative messianic beliefs rooted in Judaism.

To Jews such as John, for whom Jesus was still understood as the promised Jewish messiah, not as the founder of a separate religion, these more universalist Christians were an abomination. Their willingness to find accommodation with the larger Roman society was the single most divisive issue within the fledgling spiritual movement.

This earliest Christian conflict, with its roots two generations earlier in the ministry of Paul, had grown more negative and accusatory with the passage of time—particularly in the region of Asia Minor, in which prosperous cities such as Ephesus and Pergamum competed with each other in creating impressive temples to favorite Roman deities. As we shall see, it is on the Christian communities in these cities that the author of Revelation focuses his most dire warnings and threats. To him, the evil of Rome itself goes without saying. The evil that concerns and consumes him throughout his vision is the evil of those who adhere to a sort of faux-Christian faith (in his view) that exists with a fair degree of comfort within the larger energy of Rome.

So we have an angry and bitter believer in Jesus as the Jewish messiah, isolated perforce from the Roman Empire in which he lived, and isolated equally from the prevailing consciousness of his own fellow Christians. He is convinced that he is upholding, almost singlehandedly, a standard of spiritual purity and moral judgment that is the absolute prerequisite for ultimate admission to the kingdom of heaven. Substitute "American" for "Roman" and you have, I think, a fairly accurate description of many "Left Behinders" who continue to wait for John's fiercely negative vision to express in the world today.

I find it interesting that visionaries of all faiths tend to receive and share visions that exactly correspond to their own innate beliefs. That doesn't necessarily negate the power and value of the visions; but it does require us to recognize that the predisposition of the visionary plays an important role. It's not always true, of course; the singular vision of Saul of Tarsus, for example, turned his worldview completely on its head, as a Christ persecutor became a Christ believer. But it can be seen, I think, that John of Patmos' own angry judgments against more accommodating Christians played a significant role in the tone and detail of his Revelation.

The Revelation to John was accepted into the canon—that is, declared an official book of the Bible—at the Council of Carthage in 397. It was by no means a unanimous decision; in fact, many branches of Christianity continued to reject it for many years. A group of bishops led by Gregory of Nazianzus argued against including it because (prophetically enough) they felt it was too hard to understand and presented grave risks of abuse and intolerance. Even today the Eastern Orthodox Church, while including the book as Scripture, does not read from it in its liturgical calendar—the only book of the Bible to be so excluded.

It's interesting to note that Martin Luther rejected the Revelation to John early in his ministry. Later, however, he changed his mind when he found that its scary imagery of the devouring Beast could usefully be applied against the Church of Rome. The Church of Rome, of course, returned the favor, seeing itself as the good guy and placing the black hat of the Beast on Luther. This has been true of the Revelation throughout its entire history; the "correct" interpretation depended entirely on the viewpoint of the interpreter.

What ultimately argued in favor of its inclusion in the Bible, really, was the simple fact that it had become very popular. People liked it, and the church leaders reluctantly went along. Many people in the ensuing two millennia have wished it had been excluded, with its dualistic and terrifying images of eternal punishment and divine revenge. Others continue to embrace it with the same enthusiasm that made it a "best-seller" in its day.

From a metaphysical perspective—and a literary one, as well—the Revelation to John does in fact bring the long drama of the Bible to a significant and satisfactory conclusion. As we will see, some of its closing images would seem to suggest that its position as the final book is a perfect example of divine order.

Let's take a moment to clear up any confusion about the title. The author himself did not provide a title for the composition. It is usually included in English Bibles as the Revelation to John. It is also known as the Book of Revelation or as the Apocalypse, from the Greek word *apokalupsis*, which means (Duh!) "revelation."

So Apocalypse, Book of Revelation, Revelation to John— they are all acceptable titles for the same 22 chapters. I tend to use them interchangeably; don't let that throw you. Please note that the book should *never* be referred to in the plural, as Revelations. (For some reason, this particular mistake causes many Bible scholars to foam at the mouth and generally go nuts.)

There is a whole genre of writings known as apocalyptic literature, of which the Revelation is certainly a prime example. (There are others in the Bible, especially in Hebrew Scripture, including Daniel, Ezekiel and parts of Isaiah.) Apocalyptic literature is always highly symbolic and centers on revealing information that had previously been hidden, often as the result of a visionary journey to a higher realm.

The Revelation to John consists of 22 chapters. There is an underlying structure of sorts—each chapter takes us another step further into the confusing blend of spiritual truth and mortal illusion that constitutes the landscape of our personal journeys. But these steps are in no way linear or logical. Images circle back on themselves, some episodes are revisited from different perspectives, and the basic journey is interrupted at its darkest points with quiet interludes that provide a release from the stress and a ray of hope for the outcome.

There is more helpful information about the Revelation that we will explore as we delve into the text. I'll be adding periodic meditations to help us stay focused on spiritual truth, undistracted by confusing temporal images. So let's take a deep breath—and plunge in!

MEDITATION

In approaching the Revelation to John, I choose to call upon my divine gifts of appreciation, love and wisdom. My mind and my heart are open to receive the guidance and spiritual support its words may offer, and the gift of divine discernment allows me to see and claim the assurance of universal love beneath all appearances of duality and resistance.

Step 1

HEEDING THE CALL

Every revelation requires that we be "lifted" out of our day-to-day focus on the challenges and events of human existence. We cannot hear a message from the realm of Spirit if we are unaware that such a dimension exists. For Paul and later Christian mystics, the lifting is described as an experience in consciousness. John of Patmos adopts the imagery of Isaiah, Ezekiel and other Jewish prophets who describe the overwhelming beauty and power of the throne room of God.

> "The revelation of Jesus Christ, which God gave him to show his servants what must soon take place; he made it known by sending his angel to his servant John, who testified to the word of God and to the testimony of Jesus Christ, even to all that he saw. Blessed is the one who reads aloud the words of the prophecy, and blessed are those who hear and who keep what is written in it; for the time is near.
>
> John to the seven churches that are in Asia: 'Grace to you and peace from him who is and who was and who is to come, and from the seven spirits who are before his throne, and from Jesus Christ, the faithful witness, the firstborn of the dead, and the ruler of the kings of the earth.'"
>
> —Rev. 1:1-5

Who is Jesus Christ? In what way is this revelation his? It's important to note that he is not the instigator of the drama about to unfold—the vision does not come *from* Jesus. Nor is Jesus "him who is and who was and who is to come," since he (Jesus) is mentioned separately in the same list. He is a "faithful witness" whose testimony joins and supports the testimony of John, the author of the Revelation. In describing him as "the firstborn of the dead," the author suggests that Jesus is not unique in his relationship to God—or to the rest of humankind. He is rather the first to do what we all must do—move through the resistance of fear and the illusion of death to assume our spiritual role in the new consciousness that is "the kingdom of heaven." Jesus is "the ruler of the kings of the earth," not because he has armies or temporal power, but because his perfect demonstration of spiritual principle allows him to express the infinite Power of God. We are all called to achieve that same level of spiritual expression: "What I have done, you will do" (Jn. 14:12).

> "To him who loves us and freed us from our sins by his blood, and made us to be a kingdom, priests serving his God and Father, to him be glory and dominion forever and ever. Amen. Look! He is coming with the clouds; every eye will see him, even those who pierced him; and on his account all the tribes of the earth will wail. So it is to be. Amen."

—Rev. 1:5-7

It is not merely Jesus of Nazareth who is "coming with the clouds;" it is the Christ Consciousness that Jesus achieved and perfectly expresses. Everyone contains that Christ Consciousness—even those who deny and resist it. We are all inseparably one with the infinite Power and Love of God, and one with each other as the Christ of God in expression. There

will be resistance—that's what so much of the revelation is to
be about—but there can be no doubt that Christ Consciousness
will prevail, and its expression as the "kingdom of heaven" will
be achieved, because "it is to be."

> "'I am the Alpha and the Omega,' says the Lord God,
> who is and who was and who is to come, the Almighty."
>
> —Rev. 1:8

"The Lord God" is not the Allness of God as Source, but
rather the Christ of God present in each of us—"the Lord of
your being," a term used frequently in the Hebrew Scriptures.
The Christ is the Word of God. ("In the beginning was the Word,
and the Word was with God, and the Word was God. ... In him
was life, and the life was the light of all people" [Jn. 1:1, 4].) The
Christ—our own true identity—is as eternal as the Allness of
God from which it flows. It is past, present and future. We must
fully understand this about ourselves before we can proceed on
our journey into higher consciousness.

> "I, John, your brother, who share with you in Jesus the
> persecution and the kingdom and the patient endur-
> ance, was on the island called Patmos because of the
> word of God and the testimony of Jesus. I was in the
> spirit on the Lord's day, and I heard behind me a loud
> voice like a trumpet saying, 'Write in a book what you
> see and send it to the seven churches, to Ephesus,
> to Smyrna, to Pergamum, to Thyatira, to Sardis, to
> Philadelphia, and to Laodicea.'"
>
> —Rev. 1:9-11

"The persecution" of fear-based resistance to spiritual principle, "the kingdom" of fully realized Christ Consciousness, and
"the patient endurance" it takes to move *through* the resistance
to achieve and express the kingdom—these three elements are

the essence of the Revelation. Jesus clearly and lovingly demon-strated that we are to do that by remembering and expressing our spiritual powers as we work with the challenges of this human experience.

This new awareness must be activated in every aspect of our mortal identity. Every part of us—body, mind and spirit—must receive the news, which is the metaphysical purpose under-lying the symbolic seven letters. From John's perspective, the Christian communities in these seven prominent cities were committing a grievous sin in their willingness to coexist and compromise with the Roman society that surrounded them. They needed to be forcefully awakened to the absolute priority of their spiritual purpose. The same is true for us; distracted by this human experience, we lose sight of the spiritual work we are here to do. We must awaken the seven chakras—the points of powerful contact between the human and divine within us—in order to fully embrace our Hero's Journey.

> "Then I turned to see whose voice it was that spoke to me, and on turning I saw seven golden lampstands, and in the midst of the lampstands I saw one like the Son of Man, clothed with a long robe and with a golden sash across his chest. His head and his hair were white as white wool, white as snow; his eyes were like a flame of fire, his feet were like burnished bronze, refined as in a furnace, and his voice was like the sound of many waters. In his right hand he held seven stars, and from his mouth came a sharp, two-edged sword, and his face was like the sun shining with full force."
>
> —Rev. 1:12-16

The number seven will be our constant companion as we move through this revelation. We'll discuss its significance a bit later, at the end of this chapter.

"Son of Man" is a term Jesus used frequently—not simply to refer to himself, but to describe each of us. It's a translation of the Aramaic *barnasha* or "human being." It is the true spiritual identity of each of us—not limited, finite and weak, but strong, clear and radiant. Our Christ nature is pure, bright and deeply centered. It contains the seven stages (stars) of spiritual completion, and the sharp discernment (sword) necessary to cut *SWORD* through illusion and embrace the truth.

This vision of the Christ is, I think, the true touchstone of the entire Revelation. The long robe and sash denote temporal authority; the hair and eyes are radiant with divine Light. The feet are not airy and ethereal, but formed of earthly minerals, burnished and refined to reflect the Light of Spirit, and to anchor it firmly in this human dimension. It is not simply a spiritualized expression of Jesus Christ, but of each one of us— the Christ that is the true reality of every person.

> "When I saw him, I fell at his feet as though dead. But he placed his right hand on me, saying, 'Do not be afraid; I am the first and the last, and the living one. I was dead, and see, I am alive forever and ever; and I have the keys of Death and of Hades.'"
>
> —Rev. 1:17-18

Our innate Christ nature is *dead* as long as we remain ignorant of its presence. Once we recognize and embrace the Christ— the eternal Spirit that is our true identity—then we have control over the illusions of suffering and death. They will not necessarily leave us immediately—many adventures and challenges lie before us yet—but we will no longer see ourselves as their helpless victims.

In the popular and engaging saga of *Harry Potter* written by J.K. Rowling, Harry learns the truth of who he is very early on. "You're a wizard, Harry Potter," the giant Hagrid informs him on his 10th birthday, in the first book. Exciting news—but it's just the beginning of the story. He will have to learn to believe in his power, to express it effectively, and to move past the resistance to it that will arise in the world around him. It's the same for us; this vision of the Christ is exciting and reassuring, but it's not a "happily ever after" moment. Now that we see the full Christ potential in all its power and radiance, we must learn how to claim it, express it and fully become the creative spiritual beings we truly are.

> "Now write what you have seen, what is, and what is to take place after this. As for the mystery of the seven stars that you saw in my right hand, and the seven golden lampstands: the seven stars are the angels of the seven churches, and the seven lampstands are the seven churches."

—Rev. 1:19-20

The Revelation now turns to seven letters to seven early churches, located on the coast of Asia Minor in present-day Turkey. This is a good time to turn our attention to the number seven—which obviously holds great importance to the author.

Indeed, seven is a number of universal spiritual significance. It represents the cycle of spiritual awareness that we—spiritual beings in human forms—move through again and again as we proceed to fulfill our inherent purpose: creating "the kingdom of heaven" by using human challenges as opportunities to make creative spiritual choices.

In Christianity these seven stages are symbolized in the seven sacraments that mark the beginning (baptism) and ending (extreme unction) of a human experience, along with five essential stages of spiritual growth in between. In Hinduism they become the seven chakras—locations within our physical density that represent our closest links to the divine. The mystical Jewish tradition of kabala describes a Tree of Life containing 10 elements, grouped on seven distinct levels. In the first version of Creation described in the biblical Book of Genesis, we have the seven days of creation. In each case, the reference is to a process according to which divine ideas—the Christ essence eternally emanating from Divine Mind—move through us into expression in the world around us.

Once we are awakened to the Christ Presence that is our true nature, we must allow that Presence to awaken every part of our bodies and minds—all seven stages of our human expression—so that we can successfully undertake the journey that lies ahead. The seven letters that follow serve as a kind of meditation guide, helping us to recognize and awaken the strength of each stage, and begin to dissolve the problems that have accrued because we've forgotten these spiritual powers within us.

It is often helpful to visualize this essential process as a movement *upward* through the seven chakras, from a sense of being limited to this human experience to a full expression of the spiritual power that we truly embody.

Thoughts on Step 1: Heeding the Call

This "calling" that John describes may seem extraordinary, but it really isn't. Every one of us is called to experience our own personal revelations. In fact, we are called many times in the course of a human lifetime.

We may not recognize it at first as a call. Or we may do our very best to ignore it. It feels totally out of sync with the normal rhythms and concerns of life; it's not realistic. What would other people think? How could we justify to others something so strange we can barely believe it ourselves?

We can't justify it to others, of course. A divine revelation does not obey logical rules, and its purpose has nothing to do with the opinions of other people. It's an unexpected interruption in the normal flow of life, lifting us to a higher perspective so we can fully appreciate the entire creative process that is our spiritual purpose as we move through mortal challenges.

Such a revelation moment may occur when we are feeling particularly lost and alone, trapped in human addictions and fear-based dramas from which there seems to be no escape. The revelation won't solve our problems; when it's over, we'll find ourselves back in the same situation. But somehow the sense of total despair that had been weighing so heavily upon us is dissolved, and a way forward seems, if not easy, at least possible.

The first revelation I recognized as such (albeit somewhat foggily) in my own life occurred when my physical body was in an intensive care unit, desperately ill—dying, in fact, from all the physical damage we can do to ourselves when we allow addictions to completely rule our lives. In my case, they were alcohol and drugs. While I was ostensibly in a coma for more than a week, my consciousness was far from asleep. I was experiencing a revelation as dramatic as John's (but without all the gory stuff).

In my revelation, I could recognize the pain in the body beneath me, but I was free of it. I knew I was near death, and I was fine with that. I was eager to leave my human form behind and move on. I had an awareness that I had somehow failed to accomplish something, but I didn't care. The pain and despair were gone at last; I felt safe and blissfully happy. That was enough.

But no; I was told I had to go back. There was work I had committed to do, and it had to be done. I was very reluctant, but my spirit guides were equally as insistent. Like John's, my revelation included a solemn assurance: If you go back, I was promised, things will never again be as unbearable as they had been.

That was in 1974. Since then I have been through as many challenges, dramas, conflicts, fears, shadows and sheer pain as—I imagine—you have been. There have certainly been times when I've wanted to cry foul and remind Someone of that promise. Yet I have not surrendered to my addictions from that day to this. Somehow, the total despair I felt at that time has never returned. I have often felt lost and in pain; but I have never felt abandoned and hopeless.

So revelations can come—as John's apparently did—from a time of darkness and confusion, offering a vision of hope and reassurance. Often it's only when we have painted ourselves into a spiritual corner—with no way out apparent to our mortal minds—that we become reluctantly willing to hear the quiet, revelatory voice of Spirit within us. That's why, faced with the inevitable challenges, fears and resistance of my human journey, my constant prayer has become simply, *Show me the good!* That willingness is all that's necessary for the Christ perspective to transform the challenge into a creative opportunity.

Revelations can also arise from times of seductive comfort and apparent normalcy, when our physical and emotional needs are being met and we are feeling more than a little pleased with ourselves—complacent about having a firm handle on things. Their purpose then is to jolt us awake from our self-imposed stupor of comfort, and to remind us that we aren't here in human form to be comfortable. We're here to be creative—to make the challenging choices that will bring the new dimension of spiritual consciousness—the kingdom of heaven—into expression.

My life was going quite well some eight years after that first revelation. My theater work had taken me from New York City to Chicago, and I was having success as actor, director and playwright. I was happy, for sure, but there was a shadow of dissatisfaction beneath the happiness. I found my way to Unity about this time, and began taking classes and being of service and—in the eyes of everyone but me—moving clearly toward ministerial school. I knew such an idea was absurd, but I played along to a certain extent. I took a few classes at Unity Village in Missouri, sent in an application when the time came, went through the interview process and, to my utter astonishment, was accepted!

Well, I certainly wasn't going to go! I had a very nice life—a lovely apartment, a fun social life, and directing assignments lined up for months to come. This is what I had always wanted! I was not letting it go.

But the strangest things began to happen. The theater that had booked me to direct three productions suddenly went bankrupt. No work. My apartment building was sold and going condo. No home. People in my social life seemed to forget I was still around. It felt as though I had already taken leave of my own former life—and I was the only one who didn't know it! Finally, one night, I was awakened out of a sound sleep by a voice as loud and clear as John's was to him. Scared me half to death! It said—and I quote—"Beloved, will you leave all this and follow me?"

Somehow trying to argue or bargain did not feel appropriate. So I squeaked out a tentative "Yes?" and that's all it took. Within a month I had moved to Unity Village and found a job in the Silent Unity prayer ministry, from which I was able to sit for hours with an elevated perspective and wonder, What on earth had happened to my best-laid plans?

The point is that these revelation experiences, whether they lift us from pain or jolt us from complacent comfort, have a single purpose. They remind us of our spiritual truth, our spiritual identity, and they seek to restore the awareness of, and enthusiasm for, our spiritual work to do that we once had when we signed on for this human adventure.

MEDITATION

I AM open and receptive to the guidance of Spirit in every area of my human experience. I ask without doubt or fear for the revelation of spiritual Truth that will show me my next steps. I AM deeply grateful for the love and trust in which every true revelation is shared. Thank you, God!

Questions for Discussion

1. Can you remember a time when you may have chosen to ignore a call to revelation—an invitation to rise above human pain or comfort and learn more about your spiritual purpose? As you look back on it, what was the result?

2. Have you ever accepted a call to revelation? How did the call express? What was its implied promise? How did the experience affect your life afterwards?

3. Simply choosing to explore this Revelation to John suggests that you are open and willing for further revelations in your own consciousness. The infinite energy of the Divine will respond to that willingness. What do you hope to receive out of future revelations as they occur?

Step 2

AWAKENING LOWER CHAKRAS

N ow that our Christ nature has our attention, the next essential step is to bring our full human expression into spiritual alignment. After all, a revelation is only necessary when we have forgotten the spiritual Truth of who we are and what we are in human form to accomplish.

This "forgetting" is not just a mental lapse; it has affected every dimension of our human experience. Like Dorothy Gale in the poppy fields of Oz, we have lost every sense of spiritual identity and creative purpose. We must become fully awake in order to remember—and to resume our spiritual journey.

In the Revelation to John, this awakening process is metaphysically described in terms of letters to seven spiritual centers on Asia Minor that have, in John's opinion, lost their way through heretical compromise and coexistence with other religious and political energies.

> "To the angel of the church in Ephesus write: These are the words of him who holds the seven stars in his right hand, who walks among the seven golden lampstands:
>
> 'I know your works, your toil and your patient endurance. I know that you cannot tolerate evildoers; you have tested those who claim to be apostles but are not, and have found them to be false. I also know that you are enduring patiently and bearing up for the sake of my name, and that you have not grown weary.

But I have this against you, that you have abandoned the love you had at first. Remember then from what you have fallen; repent, and do the works you did at first. If not, I will come to you and remove your lampstand from its place, unless you repent. Yet this is to your credit: you hate the works of the Nicolaitans, which I also hate.'"

—Rev. 2:1-6

The first stage we experience as we bring our spiritual identity into a mortal body and human experience concerns the group—the tribe, the family—with which we associate ourselves in earliest consciousness. It is represented by Ephesus— one of the most worldly of cities, caught up with its pre-eminent role in the Roman Empire. As a chakra, this stage is centered in the coccyx—the base of the spine. As a sacrament, it is baptism—a process by which our innate spirit is welcomed into a human community and given the name by which we will be known.

This stage includes some of the basics of the human experience—patient endurance, hard work. It's important that we be solidly grounded in our humanity before our spiritual purpose begins to express, and this stage is committed to that need. It's also important to realize that the density of the human experience—especially as expressed in our individual bodies—is not an enemy of spiritual purpose. We must be comfortable with these "earth suits" in order to proceed effectively on our journey.

The challenge at each of the seven stages is that we may come to believe that the stage is the only reality, rather than a part of a larger process. We may become so comfortable in our humanity that we forget there's more to us than that. We lose the spiritual energy and enthusiasm with which we undertook this great journey.

Since we will encounter the word often in the pages ahead, it's important to understand at the outset what *repent* suggests at its deepest, metaphysical level. It shares a linguistic root with words such as *pensive* and *penitent*. That root refers to the process of thought. To repent is to think again—to recognize a false thought that is impeding our spiritual progress and to replace it with a true thought, anchored in our Christ energy. There is no guilt, shame or punishment involved in this process of *repentance*—unless we choose to put it there. It is simply the replacement of a false thought with a spiritual truth. We *deny power* to the false—we "unplug" the thought in consciousness—and we *empower* a new understanding that is expressive of whom we truly are.

So "repent, and do the works you did at first" calls us to remember and express the spiritual energy and enthusiasm with which we undertook this great adventure. The "Nicolaitans" were a Christian sect that retained pagan practices. In resisting their energy, we are affirming that this spiritual journey cannot move forward through compromise with human distractions. It's only by surrendering completely to the Christ within that the pleasures of the human experience can be appreciated in a proper co ntext.

> "Let anyone who has an ear listen to what the Spirit is saying to the churches. To everyone who conquers, I will give permission to eat from the tree of life that is in the paradise of God."
>
> —Rev. 2:7

"The tree of life" will be another recurring image as the Revelation continues to unfold. It takes us back to the very earliest pages of the Bible—the third chapter of Genesis, in which Adam and Eve are sent from the Garden of Eden.

At that time, "cherubim and a flaming sword" (Gen. 3:24) are placed around the tree of life to prevent mankind from approaching it. This is not a punishment, but a loving safeguard. Eating from the tree of life at too early a stage in our journey into the appearances of duality would lock us forever in those appearances, making the illusion real. We need to be protected from the tree of life until we are ready in consciousness to end our adventures and claim the kingdom of heaven. We'll discuss this further when the image reappears. For now it's enough to remember that this possibility exists as a promise that unfolds as we move forward.

> "And to the angel of the church in Smyrna write: These are the words of the first and the last, who was dead and came to life:
>
> 'I know your affliction and your poverty, even though you are rich. I know the slander on the part of those who say that they are Jews and are not, but are a synagogue of Satan. Do not fear what you are about to suffer. Beware, the devil is about to throw some of you into prison so that you may be tested, and for ten days you will have affliction. Be faithful until death, and I will give you the crown of life.
>
> Let anyone who has an ear listen to what the Spirit is saying to the churches. Whoever conquers will not be harmed by the second death.'"
>
> —Rev. 2:8-11

At the second stage, our focus shifts from who we are as part of a group—a tribe, a community, a family—to who we individually are *within* that group, and how we relate to others in the group. This is the process that the great psychiatrist Karl Jung called "individuation." We begin to explore, not just who we are as a part of the great collective I AM, but who we individually are, and how we uniquely contribute to the whole.

The strengths we can already realize within ourselves, even at this early stage of the journey, include a strong survival instinct—the ability to sustain loss and disappointment and continue forward nonetheless. The danger of being distracted at this level is that we may come to believe that "affliction and poverty" are meant to be our lot in life. We may become quite adept at combating them, but doing battle *against* these negative energies may actually contribute to our belief in their reality.

"Life is hard and then you die" is perhaps the ultimate Smyrna-esque statement. From the perspective of Christ awareness, we see that life is indeed hard. Affliction and poverty are parts of the human experience, but they are not its reality. The reality is that "we are rich." The challenges we encounter are there so that we can create the kingdom—"the crown of life"—by moving through them, transforming them with our innate spiritual energies.

This is the "middle path" that is the essence of our spiritual journey—not denying the suffering and challenges that we encounter, nor surrendering to them as the victims we once believed ourselves to be, but experiencing challenge from a Christ-centered understanding of the creative possibilities it represents.

> "And to the angel of the church in Pergamum write: These are the words of him who has the sharp two-edged sword:
>
> 'I know where you are living, where Satan's throne is. Yet you are holding fast to my name, and you did not deny your faith in me even in the days of Antipas my witness, my faithful one, who was killed among you, where Satan lives.

> But I have a few things against you: you have some there who hold to the teaching of Balaam, who taught Balak to put a stumbling block before the people of Israel, so that they would eat food sacrificed to idols and practice fornication. So you also have some who hold to the teaching of the Nicolaitans. Repent then. If not, I will come to you soon and make war against them with the sword of my mouth.
>
> Let anyone who has an ear listen to what the Spirit is saying to the churches. To everyone who conquers I will give some of the hidden manna, and I will give a white stone, and on the white stone is written a new name that no one knows except the one who receives it.'"

—Rev. 2:12-17

The process of individuation continues in this third stage, as we move beyond separating our sense of self from the larger group and begin to learn more about who we are and how we're meant to express. This requires an energy of self-esteem and self-confidence. As a chakra, it is centered in the solar plexus—where we can painfully feel things "in the gut," but where we will also find the "gut instincts" that can guide us safely through every challenge.

In her powerful book *Anatomy of the Spirit*, the wonderful teacher and author Carolyn Myss notes that, in the kabalistic tree of life, this stage is represented by the twin powers of *Nezah* (endurance) and *Hod* (integrity). They serve to both ground us in this human experience and infuse us with our own, unique spiritual guidance. It's at this level that people may experience angels or spirit guides—or a strengthening of an innate sense of relationship to the divine. Like the Christian sacrament of confirmation, the Pergamum stage represents a conscious choice to recognize, and relate to, the dimension of Spirit.

The danger at this stage is that our innate spiritual instincts may be confused by contradictory teachings—often well-meaning—that we receive from others around us. We must learn to put our own personal relationship to God ahead of all other input. That relationship will be our *hidden manna*—a source of strength, nourishment and abundance. *"I have food to eat that you don't know about,"* Jesus said to his disciples when they tried (like the Jewish mothers some of them probably were) to get him to eat a little something (Jn. 4:32). This intimate, personal relationship with the Presence within us is symbolized by the white stone on which is written a new name—your divine identity—known but to you.

> "And to the angel of the church in Thyatira write: These are the words of the Son of God, who has eyes like a flame of fire, and whose feet are like burnished bronze:
>
> 'I know your works—your love, faith, service, and patient endurance. I know that your last works are greater than the first.
>
> But I have this against you: you tolerate that woman Jezebel, who calls herself a prophet and is teaching and beguiling my servants to practice fornication and to eat food sacrificed to idols. I gave her time to repent, but she refuses to repent of her fornication. Beware, I am throwing her on a bed, and those who commit adultery with her I am throwing into great distress, unless they repent of her doings; and I will strike her children dead. And all the churches will know that I am the one who searches minds and hearts, and I will give to each of you as your works deserve. But to the rest of you in Thyatira, who do not hold this teaching, who have not learned what some call 'the deep things of Satan,' to you I say, I do not lay on you any other burden; only hold fast to what you have until I come.

> To everyone who conquers and continues to do my works to the end, I will give authority over the nations; to rule them with an iron rod, as when clay pots are shattered—even as I also received authority from my Father. To the one who conquers I will also give the morning star. Let anyone who has an ear listen to what the Spirit is saying to the churches.'"

—Rev. 2:18-29

We are now at the very center of this process of awakening the "churches"—the dimensions of spiritual awareness within us. As a chakra, the fourth stage is centered in the heart. In the creative process described in Genesis, the general light of consciousness we feel at first now becomes specific sources of light within that consciousness—and within our lives. This marks our awareness of the spiritual power of love—and of the many emotions, positive and negative, that we may experience as we endeavor to understand and express that love.

At our best, this level expresses as "love, faith, service and patient endurance." The spiritual connection we felt at the third stage is now enhanced and deepened through a higher awareness, and it becomes the basis for rich and meaningful personal relationships.

The danger of getting stuck at this stage is represented by "the woman Jezebel." John's readers would have been very familiar with the biblical story of Jezebel, wife to King Ahab, who used her power and physical allure to lead her husband—and, through him, all of Israel—away from their commitment to their God, the Lord of their beings (see 1 Kings 17 et seq.). We "tolerate the woman Jezebel" in our own lives when we allow the spiritual power of love to become polluted with human fears, resulting in distorted feelings of obsession, lust, possessiveness, jealousy or even hatred.

"Repentance" at this stage requires that we "hold fast" to the spiritual truth we have found and nurtured within ourselves and make the Christ within us our only priority. If we hold fast, we will be able to shatter the "clay pots" of distracting emotions and recognize "the morning star"—the divine light that clearly marks the path we are to travel.

Thoughts on Step 2: Awakening Lower Chakras

This step has proved to be one of the most important in terms of my own spiritual path. It serves as a vivid reminder that we cannot achieve our spiritual purpose unless we are solidly and positively grounded in our human bodies and lives.

It is tempting, once we have heard the call of revelation, to assume that we should now be dwelling solely in the upper, more ethereal realms where our true identity lies. Now that we know we are not simply our mortal selves, it seems logical that we can ignore our baser issues and instincts and focus on living in our new spiritual awareness.

It doesn't work that way, however. Our spiritual purpose is not to overcome the physical, but to transform it. If we are not at peace in our lower chakras, we will not be able to ascend in consciousness to the higher realms, and then to allow that higher spiritual energy to flow back into our human bodies and experiences.

For me, one great temptation of these lower chakras has been to believe that I need outside help to reach or understand the higher dimensions of spiritual Truth. Since I haven't yet awakened those dimensions within me, I may be vulnerable to others who have—or who believe they have! Some such "spirit guides" may be very well-intentioned. Others are more deliberately manipulative. They can be very helpful, so long as they, and I, remember always that my connection to Divine Mind is direct and immediate. Teachers or practices may help me find that connection; but no teacher or practice can ever interpret it for me.

I've had to learn that I already have within me all the wisdom and guidance I may need—I don't need to give any of my power away to an outside authority figure, whether a church, a prophet, the stars or a deck of cards. At the same time, I am open to the possibility that outer guides may help me *find* that inner knowing, so long as I keep the focus on the Christ within, and not on the messenger. It has happened from time to time that such a guide or messenger has appeared on my path, without any particular effort on my part to find one. They always seem to offer a mirror onto a part of my inner process that is very useful just at that moment.

The one consistent reminder I've received again and again is that I need to stay grounded in this human experience—centered and comfortable in my own body. I've been told by people aware of such things that my aura sort of faded out at my knees, indicating that the lower chakras are not my strong suit. I had a spiritual bodyworker spend literally months focusing on my legs, to allow spiritual energy to flow more freely all the way to my feet. And an astrologer once told me that, as a spiritual being, I was so eager to rush into human form, to be available for the work we're all here to do, that I neglected to take the time to ground myself first. As a result, from my earliest childhood, I have been much more comfortable in the upper chakras—dealing with ideas and imagination—than in the lower chakras that would allow me to comfortably negotiate human issues and experiences.

I've been reading recently that scientists are discovering that the condition known as autism is not a set of specific symptoms, but rather a wide spectrum representing varying degrees of disassociation with what are considered the benchmarks of normal human behavior. I think what they're saying is that it's neither a physical nor an intellectual condition at all. It's a question of how successfully our spiritual identity is able to be comfortable with the limitations of a human experience.

Those of us who have always been somewhat bewildered about just how the world is supposed to work, and why so many others seem to understand it better than we do, no matter how smart we may otherwise be, have simply neglected to ground ourselves. I used to think I was the only one, but as I've been willing to share my own story through the years, I've discovered there are many of us, trying with varying degrees of success to conceal how hopeless we often feel in the face of simple human challenges that others seem to just breeze through.

This is why Carolyn Myss's *Anatomy of the Spirit* has been my constant companion for many years. It has helped me understand the importance of being comfortable in my own skin— of embracing the personal identity, family relationships and communal consciousness that are so essential as a framework of strength and support, allowing me to move upward in consciousness on a firm foundation, and to allow spiritual energy to flow back in ways that are effective, efficient and practical.

The message of Step 2 then, is that this Hero's Journey we are here to accomplish requires that every chakra of our being be awake, alert and fit. Yes, the heart chakra is the center and focus of the divine energy we will experience and express. But first things first! We must be able to stand on our own feet, interact with others, and be comfortable in our physical "earth suits" before we can rise to loftier heights.

MEDITATION

In this moment I feel infinite love and appreciation for the physical body in which I AM centered and comfortable as I contemplate the joys and challenges of the human life I am experiencing. I extend that same love and appreciation to all those in my extended family who support and challenge me, allowing me to grow in strength and understanding. And I give thanks for the practical guidance to be found in the collective consciousness I share with others, and for the spiritual gift of discernment that allows me to brush aside the fear-based delusions that consciousness also contains, claiming only the wisdom and love. Thank you, God!

Questions for Discussion

1. How would you describe the family or community into which you were born? What unique challenges has that group offered on your spiritual path? What important gifts have you come to appreciate from their energy in your life?
2. In what ways have you felt yourself to be "poor" as your life has unfolded? As you look back on your experiences of poverty, what riches can you now see that weren't apparent then?
3. If "Satan's throne" represents our greatest fear, what is that fear for you?
4. On a white stone of infinite possibility, we are invited to define ourselves with a new name. What is your new name?
5. In what ways does the voice of Jezebel try to distract you from your spiritual commitment? How do you distinguish the voice of Jezebel from the voice of the Christ?

Step 3

EXPLORING HIGHER CHAKRAS

The final three letters to the churches of Asia Minor serve as a reminder that our spiritual process does not necessarily get easier as our commitment to it grows. The brighter the light, the darker the shadows. The more completely we awaken to our spiritual potential and purpose, the more resistance we can expect from those parts of our consciousness still addicted to the dualistic drama of our human existence. A "lukewarm" commitment will not be able to withstand the resistance; we must maintain our wholehearted focus on spiritual priority.

> "And to the angel of the church in Sardis write: These are the words of him who has the seven spirits of God and the seven stars:
>
> 'I know your works; you have a name of being alive, but you are dead. Wake up, and strengthen what remains and is on the point of death, for I have not found your works perfect in the sight of my God. Remember then what you received and heard; obey it, and repent. If you do not wake up, I will come like a thief, and you will not know at what hour I will come to you.'"
>
> —Rev. 3:1-3

The fifth chakra is located at the base of the tongue—in the throat and thyroid. It is the chakra of personal power, since power is expressed metaphysically by "speaking the Word." As we marshal our forces for the challenges that lie ahead, and for the creative work that is ours to accomplish, we must be willing to claim and express all of our innate spiritual power, trusting it completely to lead us where it will.

We may pay lip service to this new dimension of spiritual awareness, and we may go through the motions of putting that awareness into action. But the Power of God is not deceived. "You have a name of being alive, but you are dead." We cannot move further on our spiritual path by simply being obedient to outside guidance; we must recognize our own innate divine power, and have the faith and confidence to "wake up." Our work will not be "perfect in the sight of … God" until it force-fully expresses the Power of God within us.

> "Yet you have still a few persons in Sardis who have not soiled their clothes; they will walk with me, dressed in white, for they are worthy. If you conquer, you will be clothed like them in white robes, and I will not blot your name out of the book of life; I will confess your name before my Father and before his angels. Let any-one who has an ear listen to what the Spirit is saying to the churches."

—Rev. 3:4-6

Charles Fillmore, the American mystic and a founder of the spiritual movement known as Unity, taught that all characters in the Bible metaphysically correspond to thoughts in our con-sciousness. From that understanding, this paragraph becomes a loving warning not to "throw the baby out with the bathwa-ter." There are many thoughts in our consciousness that have not become "soiled" with the fear-based input of our mortal senses and emotions. This great spiritual journey, then, is not about finding outside of ourselves "God thoughts" that we don't contain within. The journey requires us to look within, to find those thoughts that are not soiled but purely expressive of perfect Spirit, to "clothe them in white robes" and make them our guides and inspiration.

"The book of life" is another image that will recur often as the Revelation unfolds. It cannot be a question of life as opposed to death, for death is a mortal illusion, not a spiritual truth. I think of "the book of life" as a roster of the spiritual entities (that would be us) presently engaged in this great human adventure. We can be "blotted out" of the book, not by dying, but by living our lives in ignorance of our spiritual identity and spiritual purpose. It is this spiritual ignorance that causes us to wander aimlessly through many painful life experiences, until the inevitable moment when we remember who we are and what we've agreed to accomplish together.

> "And to the angel of the church in Philadelphia write: These are the words of the holy one, the true one, who has the key of David, who opens and no one will shut, who shuts and no one opens:
>
> 'I know your works. Look, I have set before you an open door, which no one is able to shut. I know that you have but little power, and yet you have kept my word and have not denied my name. I will make those of the synagogue of Satan who say that they are Jews and are not, but are lying—I will make them come and bow down before your feet, and they will learn that I have loved you. Because you have kept my word of patient endurance, I will keep you from the hour of trial that is coming on the whole world to test the inhabitants of the earth. I am coming soon; hold fast to what you have, so that no one may seize your crown. If you conquer, I will make you a pillar in the temple of my God; you will never go out of it. I will write on you the name of my God, and the name of the city of my God, the new Jerusalem that comes down from my

God out of heaven, and my own new name. Let anyone
who has an ear listen to what the Spirit is saying to the
churches.'"

—Rev. 3:7-13

In this letter to the church in Sardis, we have released every
sense of personal weakness to affirm and express the infinite
spiritual Power that lives within us and expresses through us.
Now, at this sixth level, we recognize that the creative possibilities inherent in expressing that Power are equally infinite.

The sixth chakra is centered in the pineal gland, between the
eyes. It is, in fact, the "third eye" that allows us to perceive spiritual energy and spiritual possibility—"an open door, which
no one is able to shut." When we are first able to see through
this third eye, the perception may seem weak and tentative—as
though we have "but little power." But if we are patient with
ourselves, and steadfast in our commitment to spiritual purpose, the creative power at work through this third eye will
guide us unerringly through the dramas of human experience,
allowing us to avoid the excesses of the "hour of trial that is
coming on the whole world."

These energies—the fifth and sixth combined—require that
we release every sense of personal inadequacy or limited possibility. No matter how tumultuous the world around us may
seem as we gaze at it through our two human eyes, there is
always another way of seeing it—and of seeing ourselves.
Through the third eye of creative intention, we bring our spiritual power to bear on every challenge the world may offer, and
we allow ourselves to become the agent of transformation that
is needed.

"And to the angel of the church in Laodicea write: The
words of the Amen, the faithful and true witness, the
origin of God's creation:

"I know your works; you are neither cold nor hot. I wish that you were either cold or hot. So, because you are lukewarm, and neither cold nor hot, I am about to spit you out of my mouth. For you say, 'I am rich, I have prospered, and I need nothing.' You do not realize that you are wretched, pitiable, poor, blind, and naked. Therefore I counsel you to buy from me gold refined by fire so that you may be rich; and white robes to clothe you and to keep the shame of your nakedness from being seen; and salve to anoint your eyes so that you may see."

—Rev. 3:14-18

In awakening the first six dimensions of our innate creative energy, we have come far and accomplished much. In this final stage, we are asked to release the need for personal gain and growth, and to realize that we are engaged in this process for a much larger purpose. Our own lives will have improved by the time we reach this stage—we may feel rich and prospered in many ways. But we remain wretched and poor until we surrender to the infinitely larger purpose of transforming our shared human consciousness.

That larger purpose requires that we be fully engaged in our process of spiritual discovery. We can't be lukewarm about it—we can't settle for less than our full potential. Some people seem to think that "lukewarm" represents a desirable stage of spiritual growth—a sacred midpoint between the dualistic extremes of hot and cold. The controversial and important message here is that just the opposite is true. We are not here to find a comfortable midpoint and stay suspended between the extremes of hot and cold. We are here to fully engage those extremes, and it is when we *are* fully engaged that we are completely expressing our spiritual purpose. Our innate spiritual gold must be refined through the fire of human fears and challenges. Our sense of human "nakedness"—weakness and limitation—must be robed in the realization of our true spiritual Oneness. We must anoint our eyes with spiritual healing so that we see as God sees.

> "I reprove and discipline those whom I love. Be earnest, therefore, and repent. Listen! I am standing at the door, knocking; if you hear my voice and open the door, I will come in to you and eat with you, and you with me. To the one who conquers I will give a place with me on my throne, just as I myself conquered and sat down with my Father on his throne. Let anyone who has an ear listen to what the Spirit is saying to the churches."

—Rev. 3:19-22

The promise here is that the challenges we may encounter on our path are not signs of divine anger, signs that we're doing something wrong. They are rather expressions of divine love, a recognition that we are fully engaged in the spiritual work we're here to accomplish. Reversing one of Jesus' most vivid promises ("knock and the door will be opened"), we are asked to be, not the visitor seeking admittance, but the host. If we listen, we will hear the knock of Spirit urging us to move further in spiritual expression. If we simply open the door, all things will be possible.

John Dominic Crossan, author of *Jesus: A Revolutionary Biography* and many other powerful books on the New Testament, writes vividly about the power and importance in the Jewish society of Jesus' time of "commensality"—the sharing of communal meals. Questions of with whom one should, or should not, share a meal were of paramount importance. We see this reflected often in the ministry of Jesus; he shocked the Pharisees and other traditional thinkers by dining with prostitutes, tax collectors and many other religiously unacceptable people. So it is not surprising—and totally affirming—that

Jesus, in his full expression of the Christ, promises to mingle with us freely, and promises that as we learn to fully express the Christ within ourselves, we will become fully one with him as we are all truly One with God. That promise is complete and absolute. We simply have to listen with spiritual ears!

Thoughts on Step 3: Exploring Higher Chakras

These first three chapters of the Revelation to John are, I think, a concise and vivid overview of the process to be explored in the entire work. We are to move from a fear-based belief in limitation and unworthiness, through a creative process of awakening our innate powers and perceptions, to a full realization of our spiritual Truth, expressing as the Christ, the Lord of our individual beings, just as Jesus expressed the Christ of his being. When this process is complete, we will be one with Jesus in Christ awareness and expression, as we are all, now and always, One with the infinite Goodness that is God.

It's important to keep in mind going forward that the Revelation to John is not a linear work; it does not begin at the beginning and move logically and consistently to a conclusion. It's more like a piece of music—it introduces a number of individual but related themes, changes tone and focus many times, repeats the same passages over and over again, stating them in different ways and showing them in different lights. It's very *impressionistic*, in ways that are more clearly related to Eastern thought and literary traditions than to the more logical, orderly, intellectual approach we are accustomed to in the West.

One of the most important guides on my own spiritual journey was a therapist who refused to treat me. I don't remember his name, but I will never forget the impact of his words and choices. At the time our paths crossed, I had been involved with the Twelve Steps of recovery from addiction for just over a year. I was definitely "lukewarm" in my process. I was not indulging my addictions, which was a very good development in my life. I was making new choices—but I was making them from a rigid, strenuous application of personal will power. I was insisting on personal control of my recovery, just as I had insisted on personally controlling my time of active addiction. The idea—*any* idea—of spiritual surrender was not even a dim possibility.

If you've been through a period like that yourself, you know how incredibly painful it is. To try to make new choices while remaining defiantly immersed in old-choice consciousness is perhaps the very definition of insanity. It requires living in a state of constant vigilance. It struggles to maintain the *appearance* of recovery while refusing to acknowledge the residual power of the old consciousness. I can do this myself, my old consciousness insisted. To ask for—or even allow—help of any kind would be a sign of weakness.

After a year of this constant struggle, I found myself a patient in the psychiatric ward of a New York City hospital and, ultimately, in a state hospital situated on a remote island in the East River. This was not the result I expected from my year of "recovery," and it resulted in a full-blown clinical depression. It seemed to me proof positive that I was a victim of forces beyond my control, and I simply gave up. As I look back on that time, I can recognize a certain smug satisfaction that my darkest shadow thoughts had been right all along, and the happy endings described and celebrated in meeting rooms everywhere were not possible for the truly lost, such as myself.

I guess the therapist in question, assigned randomly to my case when I first entered the state hospital, saw the same smug satisfaction long before I could recognize it. After several tense and angry sessions in which the possibility of healing he represented did battle with my insistence on hopelessness and suicidal despair, he announced that he was taking himself off my case.

"You are certainly not going to kill yourself," he said dismissively, "because your will to live is as strong as any I have ever encountered. You're an addict, and you haven't acted on your addictions in over a year. The program has helped as much as you've allowed it, but largely it's been your own will to live. So the only question is where and how you're going to live, and that choice is entirely yours. If you choose to live here on this psych ward, shuffling around in paper slippers and eating with a spoon, fine. But I don't have the time or interest in supporting that choice; I prefer to deal with patients who are interested in recovery."

Well, I tell you, I was shocked and deeply offended. I waited a few days for him to come back and apologize. When that didn't happen, I found myself thinking about what he had said. About a week later, I went to see him. If I actually wanted to believe in the possibility of recovery, I asked, what would you suggest I do?

It was tentative and qualified, but it was at least a baby step toward recovery—toward hope instead of despair. He sent me to Twelve Step meetings on the mainland, and helped me to approach those steps as I never had before—as if they might have something to say to me. The painful intensity of maintaining a lukewarm status quo became a deep enthusiasm for the possibilities of growth and self-empowerment I began to experience as I surrendered to energies beyond my conscious control—surrendered, in fact, to the Christ energies that are my eternal identity.

I assure you there were many, many experiences of pain, resistance, arrogance and depression still to come. But something had permanently shifted. I could no longer see myself as a victim. And I could no longer insist that whatever was to be accomplished, I had to do it alone. "Alone" has not been even a faint possibility, from that moment to this.

I think this is very much where we are after three steps on the collective spiritual journey described in the Revelation. We must find it within ourselves to make the original choices that will launch us into this great drama. We must awaken and engage every aspect of our human selves through the seven universally recognized stages of spiritual awareness. The result is not that we are rewarded with power and contentment; it is that we are called to surrender our mortal process to an infinite spiritual purpose that we don't understand, and may not even believe in.

So far we've previewed and prepared for the entirety of the spiritual journey that is being revealed. But, of course, the journey is not as simple and clear-cut as this preview might suggest. There is resistance and confusion at every stage. We remember our spiritual identity and forget it and remember it again, over and over. In order to be truly useful, any spiritual revelation must recognize the dramas and conflicts that are an inevitable part of this human experience. And so this Revelation to John sets out to do just that—to describe in vivid detail the storms and conflicts we can expect at each stage of the journey.

MEDITATION

Today I choose to lift my consciousness from its lukewarm blend of fear and love to the spiritual heat of pure love. I open my heart and mind to the divine guidance of the Christ, my true spiritual identity. In the perfect love that is the Christ, I gently dissolve fear and its negative consequences as I move through this day of creative possibility.

Questions for Discussion

1. Have you ever experienced a time when you seemed very "alive" to others—successful, happy—but felt very "dead" within yourself? What was that like? What was missing? What did others not know about you that you knew about yourself?

2. What is your understanding of the "third eye"? What might a third eye allow you to see through "the open door" described in verse 8? Have you had a third eye experience yourself? What was its nature?

3. Have you ever lived through a part of your life that felt lukewarm—neither cold nor hot? What are the blessings/benefits of such a lukewarm existence? What are the negative effects?

4. "I reprove and discipline those whom I love" (verse 19). Have you ever felt the warmth of divine love, even in the midst of painful consequences of fear-based choices? How did that affect the situation at hand? Can you look back today at other challenges in which divine love seemed to be absent, and see that it was always present?

Step 4

MOVING INTO SPIRIT

We have already realized that the Revelation to John is not a logical, sequential narrative. It jumps from place to place, from image to image. And so, the seven letters having been dictated and, presumably, delivered, the Christ image vanishes and the author is presented with a new vision. It is one that would have been quite familiar to the Jewish followers of Jesus he is addressing—the throne room of God, similar to several prophetic visions from Jewish Scripture.

> "After this I looked, and there in heaven a door stood open! And the first voice, which I had heard speaking to me like a trumpet, said, 'Come up here, and I will show you what must take place after this.'"
>
> —Rev. 4:1

After the seven letters have been written and delivered—which is to say, after we have fully "spiritualized" ourselves by awakening the creative process within us—we find an open door between our limited human selves and the spiritual powers of heaven. Jesus consistently uses "heaven" to describe a realm of pure potential—the consciousness in which we recognize our innate Oneness with all that God is. Thus, in the Lord's Prayer (Mt. 6:10), he affirms "Thy will be done on earth as it is in heaven." In other words, "Let this human experience perfectly reflect and express the divine potential that is already present."

So once we have completed the seven-stage process of awakening and purification described in the letters to the seven churches, any barrier we may have felt between our limited selves and the Allness of God will dissolve. And since there is no linear timeline in the realm of Spirit—in heaven—then we will see everything clearly from that divine perspective.

> "At once I was in the spirit, and there in heaven stood a throne, with one seated on the throne! And the one seated there looks like jasper and carnelian, and around the throne is a rainbow that looks like an emerald."

—Rev. 4:2-3

Nothing is more difficult than trying to express a spiritual experience—or spiritual awareness—in terms that can be grasped by the limited human mind. The best the author could do then—indeed, the best that we can do now—is to refer and relate to images and values that have significance in our mortal world.

Since *the throne* was the recognized seat of political power in this hierarchical society, it was easy and effective to assume that the Power of God must be centered in a similar—but more magnificent—way. References to fabulous precious stones help convey the magnificence of the setting. In Ezekiel (1:26), for example, the throne is described as being made of sapphire. Here jasper, carnelian and emeralds are evoked.

> "Around the throne are twenty-four thrones, and seated on the thrones are twenty-four elders, dressed in white robes, with golden crowns on their heads. Coming from the throne are flashes of lightning, and rumblings and peals of thunder, and in front of the throne burn seven flaming torches, which are the seven spirits of God; and in front of the throne there is something like a sea of glass, like crystal."

—Rev. 4:4-6

The 24 elders represent the entire span of Judeo-Christian religious history—the 12 leaders of the 12 tribes of Israel, and the 12 disciples of the ministry of Jesus Christ. Like seven, 12 is a consistently powerful and significant number in terms of spiritual understanding.

Twelve and its multiples—especially 144, which is 12 x 12—will appear again and again as the Revelation unfolds. In addition to its historic significance in terms of both Hebrew and Christian Scriptures, it signifies the Christ Presence of God as 12 divine powers—faith, will, understanding, imagination, power, zeal, love, discrimination, strength, elimination, order and generation—in each of us. These powers are simply a way of making the general concept of the Christ more specific, and thus easier to work with and develop. By *Christ*, we mean—to quote Charles Fillmore—"the divine idea that includes all divine ideas."

[margin notes: 12, 144, 12 Powers, Christ]

Here, though, the Christ has not yet made its specific presence known and felt. The tribal elders and disciples of Jesus hold honored places in spiritual consciousness. But we will shortly see that they cannot themselves achieve the work of creating the kingdom that is our life purpose. Something more will be required.

We, too, must honor the beliefs, teachings and traditions that have led us this far on our spiritual journey. We must now be ready to move beyond them—but only with a deep sense of appreciation for the valuable ways in which they have served us. We will receive a new clarity, symbolized by the sea of crystal-like glass. The seven torches, seven spirits—the seven dimensions we are now about to explore and master—will be revealed in the presence—and with the support—of our religious past.

> "Around the throne, and on each side of the throne, are four living creatures, full of eyes in front and behind: the first living creature like a lion, the second living creature like an ox, the third living creature with a face like a human face, and the fourth living creature like a flying eagle.
>
> And the four living creatures, each of them with six wings, are full of eyes all around and inside. Day and night without ceasing they sing, '*Holy, holy, holy, the Lord God the Almighty, who was and is and is to come.*'"
>
> —Rev. 4:6-8

These four creatures are "full of eyes in front and behind" and "all around and inside"—that is to say, they are aware of everything, from the past to the future. They represent four essential aspects of the divine. The lion is the king of beasts; he represents dominion and authority. The ox represents omnipotence ("strong as an ox"). The human face represents omniscience—God as Divine Mind. The eagle expresses omnipresence, with its ability to fly everywhere, easily and effortlessly. The symbols assure us that we are in the full presence of the divine—and, by extension, that we contain these same qualities within ourselves as the Christ of our being.

These divine attributes do not sing in praise of themselves; they do not celebrate the Allness of God represented by the throne. Rather they praise "the Lord God the Almighty"—and "Lord God" always refers to the Christ—the Presence of God in God's creation, that "was and is and is to come" according to our willingness to embrace it and express it.

> "And whenever the living creatures give glory and honor and thanks to the one who is seated on the throne, who lives forever and ever, the twenty-four

elders fall before the one who is seated on the throne and worship the one who lives forever and ever; they cast their crowns before the throne, singing, '*You are worthy, our Lord and God, to receive glory and honor and power, for you created all things, and by your will they existed and were created.*'"

—Rev. 4:9-11

God is a term we use to describe the indescribable—the infinite energy of Omniscience, Omnipotence, Omnipresence and Love that is the very essence of all of life. To recognize ourselves as One with this energy and expressive of its creative Power is to awaken to the spiritual purpose that brings us into human expression. But it is a mistake to think of God *only* as the Christ of our being. God transcends any attempt to define it. So even as we claim our "crowns" of divinity, we also recognize the greater Power—the Power of creation itself that expresses as all things.

Thoughts on Step 4: Moving Into Spirit

One of the most difficult challenges of my own spiritual journey has been coming to both clarity and comfort with God—as a word, as an idea, as an energy. I have an intuitive understanding of the Christ; in fact, it was a visceral, intuitive grasp of the Christ as described by the outstanding Unity minister Eric Butterworth on Easter Sunday, 1976, that began to shake me free of old attitudes and turn me in a new direction. The universal truth that we are all divine—as all of life is divine—and divinely creative as God is eternally creative continues to reveal new depths and implications these many years later. But there has been little hard-core resistance within me to the process of Christ exploration.

But what about God? What about the Allness of infinite divinity of which the Christ is a complete expression? What about the Being of infinite love who had been an occasional source of support in my childhood? I no longer believed in the superhuman embodiment I had been told of as a child—a sort of larger and sterner version of Santa Claus who made lists from on high, kept meticulous track of who had or had not sinned, prayed, attended Mass and accepted unquestioningly the infallibility of the Church and the Pope in all things. So I knew what God wasn't—or had ceased to be—for me. But what new understanding could replace the old?

The process of remembering our own divine nature has such a revolutionary impact on every aspect of our human lives that it's easy to become exclusively absorbed in ourselves as the Christ. And, indeed, the entire purpose of our being here in this limited human experience is to continue the process of creation *as* the Christ, choice by enlightened choice. But it's a mistake, I think, to make claiming our Christ identity our primary spiritual focus. Such a focus can all too easily lead to the kind of spiritual arrogance that has wreaked so much havoc throughout recorded history.

No, our primary spiritual principle must always be what Unity has been teaching and affirming for more than a century: *There is only one Presence and one Power active in the universe, and in my life: God the Good, Omnipotence.* We could spend many lifetimes exploring this one principle and never come to the end of its implications. There is nothing but God; nothing but an energy of infinite love always working with us to guide us in our spiritual work of bringing the kingdom of heaven into tangible expression through our creative choices.

That energy of divine love has no boundaries, no limits, no tangible form. It doesn't just hang out in a place called heaven, watching its creation from afar. It is intimately one *with* its creation. It's everywhere. It's everything. We can't stand back and admire it because (to quote James Dillet Freeman) "wherever we are, God is!"

Yet something seems to be missing from this new understanding of the divine. Sometimes omnipresence feels a lot like omni-absence. Our intuitive guidance is content with this new God, and our intellect can be very happy wrestling with it. But our feelings and senses feel left out—and they need to be part of this journey too.

I've already indicated that my path into ministerial school was, to put it mildly, a bumpy one. I tried every excuse I could think of to justify refusing to go, only to have each excuse in turn dissolved in an energy that seemed to have taken possession of my mind.

The resistance and ensuing bumpiness did not disappear once my ministerial training began. Far from it. I had my suitcases at least half packed throughout my entire first year. I was convinced that at any moment either I or Unity School would realize how absurd this whole idea was, and I would either escape or be sent packing.

The more I tried to understand the spiritual principles I was presumably going to spend my life affirming, the more lost, confused and angry I felt. I had come to Unity in the first place because it seemed to offer an assurance that I wasn't crazy— that my innate spiritual guidance had worth and validity. Now it seemed clear to me that Unity itself was totally crazy. I could not go one step further on this nutty path that was unfolding before me. And neither could I go back to the comfortable old victim consciousness in which nothing was my fault, so there was nothing for me to do but suffer—and complain.

One afternoon, after thrashing my way through some Fillmore text or another, I went to see my metaphysics teacher, Rev. Leona Evans (Leona Stefanko at that time). I loved her class, even though it was the source of my depression and despair. But I thought that she, if anyone, would understand why it was impossible for me to stay in school one more day. She listened patiently as I explained that I had to leave ministerial training because I no longer believed in God. I had believed in *something* when I started, but that belief had been totally trashed somewhere along the line, and I was left with an empty void that would definitely not be an acceptable topic for Sunday sermons.

There was much more—I remember rambling on at great length in my attempt to communicate how absurd it was to ever think that I could become a minister. When I had finally run out of either breath or ideas, Leona smiled her truly annoying smile and said, "That void is an essential step, Ed. You're exactly where you *should* be on your path."

I have since come to realize that "You're exactly where you're meant to be" is the perfect counseling response to everything from a New Thought perspective. One might almost call it a cop-out, if one were being unkind. But at the time it seemed profound and true, and I felt one more possible escape hatch slamming shut behind me.

The point is, we need a sense of God as infinite Power at least as much as we need the more intimate realization of God as our own true identity. We don't want to hang onto God as an angry, judgmental authority figure. But we do want—we need—the sense of awe and wonder we feel as we contemplate the majesty of the infinite. Our human focus must be on the Christ—the expression of God that each of us uniquely is. But our spiritual focus requires that our senses and our feeling nature always remind us of the measureless love and eternal support in which we live and move and have our being.

So our spiritually engaged intellect may dismiss Chapter 4 of Revelation—with its images of thrones and jewels and tangible expressions of power and majesty—as Old Thought, rooted in mythology of God as a tangible king. But our senses and feelings understand and appreciate what the author is attempting to communicate—the thrilling splendor and infinite mystery that accompanies our every effort to "know God."

MEDITATION

I appreciate all the teachings, challenges and opportunities that have led me to this very point in my spiritual progress. I release all resentment and fear related to my past. I stand in this moment with an open mind and loving heart, eager to build upon all that has gone before.

Questions for Discussion

1. Have you ever felt called to "Come up here"? At what point in your journey did the call occur? How did it happen? What was the result?

2. What is the religious tradition (the 24 thrones) that directed you in the early stages of your spiritual journey? What negative energies caused you to leave that tradition behind? What can you now appreciate about that tradition that has helped you stay centered on the path?

3. If we understand the "four living creatures" to symbolize ways in which the energy of the divine expresses in our human experience, what qualities in your life could be represented by the lion, the ox, the man and the eagle? How might you relate them to the Twelve Powers of your Christ nature?

Step 5

OPENING THE SCROLL

S
o far our unfolding drama has a vivid setting, some interesting characters—and no plot. The story begins to unfold
in Chapter 5. Like our own human adventures, it begins
with an apparently clear-cut challenge. Also like our own
human adventures, it quickly gets very, very complicated. We
learn that even the simplest of choices can unleash astonishing
expressions of negative energy.

> "Then I saw in the right hand of the one seated on the
> throne a scroll written on the inside and on the back,
> sealed with seven seals; and I saw a mighty angel pro-
> claiming with a loud voice, 'Who is worthy to open the
> scroll and break its seals?'"
>
> —Rev. 5:1-2

Again with the sevens! And this particular imagery of seven
seals will carry us through the next four chapters (with a lot of
subsidiary "sevens" to be sure we get the point).

It's important to remember the awareness with which we
started. The Revelation to John does not unfold according to a
linear plotline of "this happened, and then that happened, and
then another thing happened." After all, what is being revealed
is nothing less than our spiritual purpose—the creative process
by which we are to make the choices, to be the intermediaries
through whom the spiritual power of "heaven" is brought into
expression on this human plane.

Is it your experience that life is a two-dimensional, linear progression of events? Sure, it's possible to define a timeline showing when we graduated from high school and got a job and fell in love and fell out of love and moved from one life experience to another. But we are infinitely more complicated than that! We move (sometimes "stumble" might be the better word) forward in spiritual understanding and expression. Then we forget or get distracted, and we fall back. Then the process repeats—again and again, until we despair of ever making significant progress.

The truth is, we're *always* making significant progress. We may find ourselves facing the same challenges and mistakes again and again. But we ourselves are not the same each time! We grow and learn, and while we may move through some of the same negative energies, we move through more quickly, and with greater awareness. This can be painful, but it's also progress.

And so this great Revelation mirrors our own lives. After all, there are only seven simple steps to the creative process we're here to express. It shouldn't take 22 chapters to cover them, any more than it should take us long human lifetimes to realize and master them. But we don't proceed forward in a linear fashion, as if we're working toward a degree. We rise up and down; we stumble forward and slide backward; we learn valuable lessons and promptly forget them; we wander off the clearly marked road into dense thickets of human distractions. So our basic, seven-step creative process has to appear and reappear, at different times and in different forms.

So it is that we move through the seven stages again, at a deeper level this time, symbolized by the opening of a scroll with seven seals. Our first expression of this creative process had such positive results, especially compared to the painful and limiting lives that preceded it, that we may relax into a sense of overconfidence. *I've got the hang of this now,* we say to ourselves. *I think I'll put things on cruise control for a while.* And suddenly we're in the midst of another crisis, wondering how that could possibly have happened. We have more work to do. And this time the choices we make will have more power because we are more conscious. They will arouse far more resistance from the shadowy energies of fear in which most of the world continues to live.

> "And no one in heaven or on earth or under the earth was able to open the scroll or to look into it. And I began to weep bitterly because no one was found worthy to open the scroll or to look into it. Then one of the elders said to me, 'Do not weep. See, the Lion of the tribe of Judah, the Root of David, has conquered, so that he can open the scroll and its seven seals.'"

—Rev. 5:3-5

The scroll contains the secret that will open wide the doors of the kingdom of heaven—the new consciousness that brings spiritual potential into tangible expression in this human experience. Simply reaching the scroll is a great accomplishment; it has required us to awaken our spiritual powers at all seven levels of awareness.

The traditions and teachings of our religious past have played significant roles in guiding us this far. We have seen the 24 elders representing that past seated in positions of honor around the throne of divinity. But they cannot lead us further; they cannot open the seal.

Jesus Christ—who is himself rooted in that religious and tribal history—opens the seal because he has conquered the belief in separation and limitation that holds us back. This doesn't make him unique—just first! It doesn't mean he's done the work for us. We will each have to open our own seven seals.

"Then I saw between the throne and the four living creatures and among the elders a Lamb standing as if it had been slaughtered, having seven horns and seven eyes, which are the seven spirits of God sent out into all the earth. He went and took the scroll from the right hand of the one who was seated on the throne. When he had taken the scroll, the four living creatures and the twenty-four elders fell before the Lamb, each holding a harp and golden bowls full of incense, which are the prayers of the saints. They sing a new song: *'You are worthy to take the scroll and to open its seals, for you were slaughtered and by your blood you ransomed for God saints from every tribe and language and people and nation; you have made them to be a kingdom and priests serving our God, and they will reign on earth.'*"

—Rev. 5:6-10

"The Lamb of God, who takes away the sins of the world" is a familiar image to Catholics everywhere; it is the "Agnus Dei" recited as a part of every Mass. It's familiar to Protestants as well, and many composers have set the beseeching words to powerful and plaintive melodies. It evokes Jesus as the ultimate victim, patiently going to be slaughtered for sins—*our* sins—that he did not even commit. Shame, guilt, suffering—it's all there, in one potent image.

But does it have anything to do with who Jesus Christ is, and what his purpose was in teaching and demonstrating through the years of his earthly ministry? Well, yes—and no.

The image of Jesus as a sacrificial victim, meekly and patiently allowing himself to be slaughtered as a way of restoring us to God's good favor is offensive and, frankly, ridiculous. The idea that a God of Love would ever demand human sacrifice is one we left behind long ago, in the darkest early days of religious superstition. God Himself stops the nonsense, in the Hebrew

Bible, through the story of Abraham and Isaac—the reluctant but obedient father, the innocent son and the clear spiritual message. We must "put God first," yes, but *in consciousness,* where all creative choices are made. Slaughtering innocents is not required. Animals were still sacrificed in Jesus' time, but only in the Temple and in limited, proscribed ways and times. We eventually grew out of that superstition as well and began to realize that God responds only to the heart energy we allow into our consciousness. Outer signs like sacrificing humans or animals might appeal to our own love for drama and blood-shed, but they have nothing to do with demands from God.

Yet the fact remains that Jesus did, in fact, die a painful and humiliating death—and everything that happened to him was a part of his ministry, a part of his message to us. He did not die as a victim, however, but as an example. He went through the experience of death to help us recognize its illusionary nature. "Watch," he was saying. "Watch and learn." If we understand *sin* in its literal sense of "missing the mark," then it could indeed be said that Jesus was dying for our sins. He was moving through the death illusion so that we could learn that death has no spiritual reality. He was improving our aim so we could stop sinning—stop missing the target with choices rooted in a superstitious fear of punishment and death. So he didn't die to *atone for* our sins but to dissolve our *tendency* to sin by showing us that the death we so fear is simply an illusion.

"Then I looked, and I heard the voice of many angels surrounding the throne and the living creatures and the elders; they numbered myriads of myriads and thousands of thousands, singing with full voice, *'Worthy is the Lamb that was slaughtered to receive power and wealth and wisdom and might and honor and glory and blessing!'* Then I heard every creature in heaven and on earth and under the earth and in the sea, and all that is in them, singing, '*To the one seated on the throne and to the Lamb be blessing and honor and glory and might forever and ever!*' And the four living creatures said, 'Amen!' And the elders fell down and worshiped."

—Rev. 5:11-14

This brief, vivid paragraph offers a very clear depiction of the nature of the universe. Things are going to get very chaotic as the vision continues to unfold, so it's important, I think, to anchor ourselves in an understanding of just how the Revelation sees the whole of creation.

We've discussed the 24 elders as emblematic of the whole of religious understanding—at least in the Judeo-Christian traditions. They represent the 12 tribes of Israel and the 12 disciples of Jesus. And we've seen that the "four living creatures" are tangible aspects of the infinite Divine—pre-eminence, omnipotence, omniscience and omnipresence.

The "myriads of myriads and thousands of thousands" of angels inhabit a spiritual realm—or perhaps many spiritual realms. It is the realm from which we enter into our human experiences, and the realm to which we return when each mortal life is concluded. Like the Christ Presence in each of us, the angels are expressions of divine creative energy. They are the Allness of God in spiritual expression, just as we are the Allness of God in both spiritual and human expression.

These angels—these myriad beings who are our "siblings in spirit," like us in every way except that they have not entered into the human experience of limitation and duality (at least not at present)—are completely engaged in the joyful process of being expressions of the ineffable Divine. Part of their joy lies in supporting those of us—spiritual beings like them—who have undertaken the great creative process inherent in working through human limitations.

They are with us always, these angels. They love and appreciate the work we have undertaken in moving through illusions and challenges. They support us, they protect us, they remind us of the truth when we seem destined to forget it. They respect us too much to interfere with our process, but they encourage us to keep going. Joyfully, they celebrate every hard-won step we take forward in consciousness.

That's why they sing in praise of the great step forward represented by Jesus, whose life and ministry demonstrated the creative power of the Christ in each of us, and the illusory nature of the limitations and negative energies that we allow to distract us. Indeed, all of creation joins in singing "to the one seated on the throne and to the Lamb"—to the Source of infinite love, and to the expression of infinite love through the challenges of the human experience.

This is a universe of infinite love, joy and celebration. It cannot be threatened in any way by the illusions of negativity and conflict that we encounter in this human experience. It is a universe that always knows and affirms the spiritual Truth, and that loves and guides us through challenges to fuller and fuller expressions of that Truth in our human lives. It's important to see this image clearly, and to return to it again and again through the struggles that lie ahead.

Thoughts on Step 5: Opening the Scroll

My first sponsor in recovery was a die-hard fundamentalist when it came to the Twelve Steps; he also tended to talk (to me, at least) in the kind of annoying platitudes that could be seen on the walls of every seedy meeting room in New York City, where I was living at the time. "First Things First," "A Day at a Time," "Don't Push the River"—he refused to realize that such simplistic generalities could not even begin to apply to the complex, unique and highly dramatic life challenges that totally justified my own addictive attitudes and behavior.

One of those unique challenges involved my more or less ongoing relationship with another alcoholic. Feeling very noble—and utterly oblivious to the fact that I was using the relationship to avoid my own issues—I decided that I had to focus on my partner's sobriety. Now, not only was he not sober, he had no interest in *getting* sober; but if I had to compromise my own recovery for his sake—well, wasn't that the loving and spiritual thing to do?

In response to what seemed to me to be highly sophisticated perceptions, my sponsor trundled out another recovery cliché. "It's a selfish program," he stated flatly. My hyperactive victim consciousness was deeply shocked. Selfish? *Moi*? How could I possibly trust a program that wants me to be selfish? With a sad shake of my head, I shrugged off such unloving advice and rode off like Don Quixote to save my "significant other."

Let's just say it didn't go well, and leave it at that. Not only did I not rescue him, but I barely survived the attempt myself, dragging myself back to meeting rooms with a profound sense of having seriously underestimated the power of the negative energies within me, seeking to undermine the massive shift in consciousness that recovery was both demanding and creating. It began to dawn on me that oft-repeated clichés are oft-repeated for a very simple reason. They're true.

Why does Step 5, Opening the Scroll, remind me of that particular learning experience? I think it illustrates the truth of that same perception. This spiritual journey of which we are becoming increasingly aware is, indeed, a selfish process. It's not "selfish" in the mortal-mind sense of having all our needs and demands met at the expense of whoever gets in the way. No, it's more like the instruction we hear from a flight attendant every time we board an airplane. Concerning the possibility that oxygen may be required during an in-flight emergency, we are carefully told to put our own mask on first, before trying to help others. Selfish? Not really. It's simply a recognition that if we ourselves are oxygen-deprived, we won't be of much help to others.

Each of us has an essential role to play in a process of spiritual unfoldment that will affect every expression of life on this planet—and beyond! But if we keep our focus on that big picture, we'll either scare ourselves into a deep sense of unworthiness or exhaust ourselves trying to accomplish vast spiritual goals with inadequate human skills.

The Lamb is the least impressive figure in this chapter's depiction of the heavenly throne room. True, he symbolizes the Christ—the creative and infinitely loving divinity that is his real identity. But he has been weakened and wounded by the negative power of human belief in duality and judgment. Surely the job of opening the seals—of continuing on to the next stage of spiritual expression—could be better handled by a figure more powerful, healthy and whole.

Yet it is precisely his woundedness—his understanding of the nature of the dualistic illusion he faces—that best qualifies the Lamb for the job. And he must know that about himself—know that no superficial wounds can damage his true Christ nature—before he can step quietly and confidently forward to begin the work at hand. There is a fine line of surrender between a sense of unworthiness on the one hand and overconfidence on the other. That voice of realistic spiritual awareness lives within each of us. It can't be found in the loud voices within us left by traditional religious teaching, insisting that suffering is our purpose in life. And it isn't a part of the joyful noise of those voices within us whose affirmation of Spirit is unbalanced by a realistic awareness of the nature and challenge of duality. It is a quiet voice of infinite love, infinite patience. It does not need to shout its power, nor bemoan its fate. It represents the power to make new choices. It's within you now.

MEDITATION

I AM the Lamb of God. I AM the Christ, unique in all creation as I bring spiritual truth into human illusion. I quietly, gratefully accept my spiritual purpose, my creative work to do. As I move forward, I give thanks for all those who have gone before me, and for the support of all the spiritual beings whose love and guidance enfolds me as I move forward.

Questions for Discussion

1. "And no one in heaven or on earth or under the earth was able to open the scroll." Why do you think this is so? What prevents them from opening the scroll? Is the reason the same for those in heaven and for those on earth? Who are those "under the earth"?

2. Have you ever experienced the sort of hopelessness that caused you to "weep bitterly"? What happened? How did it feel? As you look back, what benefit did that experience offer you?

3. The main characters in this scene are surrounded by "the voice of many angels, numbering myriads of myriads and thousands of thousands." Have you experienced such angels in your life? How did they express? What was their message?

4. The angels affirm that the Lamb, as a result of his willingness to open the seals, will "receive power and wealth and wisdom and might and honor and glory and blessing." Do you think that's the Lamb's *purpose* in undertaking the challenge? Why or why not? How does this relate to Jesus' teaching that we are to "seek first his kingdom and his righteousness, and all these things shall be yours as well" (Mt. 6:33)?

Step 6

RELEASING REPRESSED ENERGIES

The drama continues in Chapter 6 of the Book of Revelation, as the quiet, wounded Lamb begins to open the seven seals in sequence. The results are somewhat unexpected. Instead of images of love and peace—which might seem reasonable for the Lamb to expect, after his suffering and endurance—we encounter one of the most vivid and enduring images from the Revelation, the Four Horsemen of the Apocalypse.

> "Then I saw the Lamb open one of the seven seals, and I heard one of the four living creatures call out, as with a voice of thunder, 'Come!' I looked, and there was a white horse! Its rider had a bow; a crown was given to him, and he came out conquering and to conquer."

—Rev. 6:1-2

Our willingness to undertake the work of opening the seven seals does have one immediate benefit. When the first seal is opened, it releases a new image of the Christ, the indwelling Presence of God, riding on a white horse. It's a strong and reassuring image.

But this is only the beginning of the process. There is more work to be done, more negative thoughts and beliefs to be dissolved, before we can turn to the Christ as the one, constant Source of light and love in our lives. The "rider" has no specificity yet; we sense the power, but we have no clear idea of exactly what the Christ might be. We have much more to learn before we can fully claim its power in our lives.

So we crown the Christ in recognition of its presence and potential. And we turn to the work at hand, knowing that our newborn awareness of this spiritual energy within us will enable us to conquer doubts, fears and false beliefs. The Christ is our constant source of faith and energy, but we are not yet ready to call upon it in full confidence. The white horse and its rider leave the scene, but they will be waiting up ahead as our journey continues. In the final chapters of the Revelation, when our understanding has been expanded, we will once again experience the white horse and its rider, leading us into the New Jerusalem of elevated spiritual consciousness and expression.

> "When he opened the second seal, I heard the second living creature call out, 'Come!' And out came another horse, bright red; its rider was permitted to take peace from the earth, so that people would slaughter one another; and he was given a great sword."
>
> —Rev. 6:3-4

We might expect that the initial appearance of Christ Consciousness would bring peace to this human experience. In fact, it makes conflict inevitable, as Jesus emphasized many times in his teachings. Our new understanding is in immediate conflict with the entrenched, fear-based beliefs that have dominated our lives—and that continue to dominant the collective consciousness of the world in which we live.

This second of the traditional Four Horsemen is usually defined as imaging the horrors of war. But however alarming its appearance, the red horse and its rider are fighting with us, not against us. We do not need to attack; but we will need to defend ourselves against the established forces in consciousness that feel threatened by the new spiritual power we are releasing. We are empowered in the Christ to stand firm, holding to our truth, until the conflict subsides.

> "When he opened the third seal, I heard the third living creature call out, 'Come!' I looked, and there was a black horse! Its rider held a pair of scales in his hand, and I heard what seemed to be a voice in the midst of the four living creatures saying, 'A quart of wheat for a day's pay, and three quarts of barley for a day's pay, but do not damage the olive oil and the wine!'"
>
> —Rev. 6:5-6

If the opening of the second seal forces us to deal with the belief in duality that causes inevitable conflict, the black horse of the third seal confronts our deeply rooted belief in lack and limitation. It is traditionally viewed as emblematic of famine, but I think that rather misses the point.

The rider on the black horse is busy weighing, dividing and assigning equivalents: "a quart of wheat for a day's pay." It expresses the belief that whatever good and abundance we receive in life must be *earned*, according to an established system of values.

The truth is that our life abundance is *innate*. As "children of God"—expressions of the infinite Good of Spirit—we contain within ourselves the potential to create everything we may need or want to support our spiritual journeys through mortal life. We can't achieve new consciousness by obeying old rules and assuming the truth of old beliefs that insist our good will be withheld until we have earned it.

So our spiritual purpose does not require that we experience and accept famine, but that we recognize and dissolve the belief in lack and judgment that expresses as a lack of sustenance in all areas of life—until we accept the greater spiritual Truth that no part of our good is ever being withheld.

"When he opened the fourth seal, I heard the voice of the fourth living creature call out, 'Come!' I looked and there was a pale green horse! Its rider's name was Death, and Hades followed with him; they were given authority over a fourth of the earth, to kill with sword, famine, and pestilence, and by the wild animals of the earth."

—Rev. 6:7-8

Opening the fourth seal releases two of the most powerful fear-based beliefs that seek to block our path to new consciousness. Certainly our fears of the terrible finality of death and the threat of eternal damnation create more of a sense of helplessness and victimization than any other beliefs we have crafted for ourselves.

It was to encourage us to move beyond these fears that Jesus Christ chose to go through the painful and public process of crucifixion as his earthly ministry drew to a close. He hoped to show us that our greatest fears are based on illusions and false beliefs. We largely missed the point, too caught up in the surface drama to recognize the deeper truth.

Certainly fear of punishment and death were very real and immediate to those early followers of Jesus to whom John addresses his Revelation. It would be foolish to pretend that an appropriate amount of faith would instantly dissolve these fears, or lift us beyond their effects. Even as we strive to clear our collective consciousness of old beliefs, a significant part of that consciousness will continue to be concerned with death and punishment—fully a quarter, according to this vision.

That's a significant percentage, of course, and that amount of fear will have a draining effect on our innate spiritual energy. But the image also suggests that 75 percent of our thoughts in consciousness instinctively know that these fearful concepts are simply illusions. As with so much in the Revelation, what seems at first to be a scary, unpleasant image is, in fact, a powerful and positive promise: However strong these forces of Death and Hell may seem to be, they will never be able to overwhelm us. On our very worst days, our consciousness contains three times more positive, love-based thoughts than the negative, fear-based counterparts that manage to seem so loud and overwhelming.

> "When he opened the fifth seal, I saw under the altar the souls of those who had been slaughtered for the word of God and for the testimony they had given; they cried out with a loud voice, 'Sovereign Lord, holy and true, how long will it be before you judge and avenge our blood on the inhabitants of the earth?' They were each given a white robe and told to rest a little longer, until the number would be complete both of their fellow servants and of their brothers and sisters, who were soon to be killed as they themselves had been killed."
>
> —Rev. 6:9-11

This imagery must have had a strong immediate impact on the first readers of this Revelation, since they themselves were being persecuted and killed because of their refusal to compromise their Christ-centered beliefs. They were expecting a Second Coming—that Jesus Christ would return to lead them triumphantly into heaven—but it hadn't happened, and many were dying without the promised vindication.

But the "Second Coming" is not about Jesus coming back to resume his work. He has completed his work. The "Second Coming" is metaphysically about each of us awakening to the same Christ Presence in us that Jesus taught and demonstrated in himself. To a certain extent that "Second Coming" will express as light and love in our individual lives as we awaken to our spiritual truth. And to a larger extent, it will require enough of us being awake to have a decisive impact on our collective consciousness.

So the message here, I think, is that there will be some bumpy times as that collective awareness painstakingly unfolds. We will walk through life in "white robes"—a newly-discovered sense of safety and security within the turmoil of the human experience. The awakened consciousness will eventually predominate, and the fear-based persecution will dissolve. In the meantime, we must feel the love of our own white robes, and be on the lookout for others displaying the white robe of awakened consciousness, so that in joining together we hasten the day of transformation.

> "When he opened the sixth seal, I looked, and there came a great earthquake; the sun became black as sackcloth, the full moon became like blood, and the stars of the sky fell to the earth as the fig tree drops its winter fruit when shaken by a gale. The sky vanished like a scroll rolling itself up, and every mountain and island was removed from its place. Then the kings of the earth and the magnates and the generals and the rich and the powerful, and everyone, slave and free, hid in the caves and among the rocks of the mountains, calling to the mountains and rocks, 'Fall on us and hide us from the face of the one seated on the throne and from the wrath of the Lamb; for the great day of their wrath has come, and who is able to stand?'"

—Rev. 6:12-17

We might expect that, as we move through the process of opening the seven seals, our path would become increasingly smooth, our lives increasingly peaceful. The Revelation wants us to recognize that this is not going to be the case. Jesus, too, went to great pains to emphasize that following his path to Christ awareness would be challenging, conflicted and scary.

This is important because, if we don't properly understand it, we can easily become frightened and discouraged when the path we thought would lead us to peace and abundance seems instead to be pulling us deeper into shadows of fear and suffering.

And so the dramatic and frightening sixth seal imagery illustrates an essential metaphysical point. As we allow more and more of our innate, divine creative power to express in our human experience, none of our previous assumptions about life will be safe. Nearly all of the beliefs we have comfortably accumulated as we've moved through life are, in fact, based in a false understanding of our true identity, and our true relationship with the Power of God. They will all be "shaken by a gale" as a new Christ awareness becomes our creative force. And everything that once seemed powerful and important—"the kings of the earth and the magnates and the generals and the rich and the powerful"—will have to be re-examined and re-evaluated in the light of our new understanding.

From the human perspective of those kings and generals, this upheaval will, indeed, seem like a "day of wrath." They will assume it to be the judgment of an angry God—an expression (in one of the most absurd images imaginable) of "the wrath of the Lamb."

That is not its truth. The upheaval is not an expression of wrath, but of empowerment. Old beliefs, old habits, old relationships, old choices must be seen through fresh eyes as the seals of ignorance open. Some of them will prove to be valuable in our new consciousness, and will accompany us as we continue our journey. Others, rooted completely in fear and limitation, will not survive the transition.

Anyone who has ever moved through the process of releasing an old addiction of any kind will intuitively understand the vivid imagery with which the Revelation describes the opening of this sixth seal. "The brighter the light, the darker the shadows." It's important to recognize the upheavals we may experience, not as warnings that we're doing something wrong, but as signs that we are doing something right. We are moving forward despite the best efforts of our fear-based old consciousness to scare us into turning back.

There is one seal left to open. But before we get to the seventh seal, the Revelation invites us to take a time-out. It offers the first of several "interludes" that provide a break from the intensity of the process, and a fresh perspective on the experience we're sharing.

Thoughts on Step 6: Releasing Repressed Energies

The underlying message of this powerful chapter, with its images of negative energy expressing in even the most well-intentioned of lives, is difficult for some to accept. It's at this point in the Revelation that many people who have painfully freed themselves from old beliefs in suffering and punishment as integral parts of our human experience close the book and go in search of something more positive and uplifting to read.

Dr. Elizabeth Cady, the 19th-century spiritual seeker and writer whose book *Lessons in Truth* has been a New Thought standard for well over a century, encountered the same resistance to a chapter in that book that described the same phenomenon—that positive, spiritually-inspired steps forward can result in a strong backlash of negative energy. She called the process *chemicalization*, and she described it calmly, without the alarm or drama found in the Revelation, as an almost reassuring sign that we are moving in the right direction. It is unavoidable, she wrote, that our efforts and intentions to claim a more positive, faith-filled basis for our human lives will be seen as profoundly threatening to feelings and thoughts rooted in the deep belief in the illusion of duality from which we are newly awakened.

Dr. Cady's chapter on chemicalization was found so troubling that it was removed from the book for many years, and through many editions. Thankfully, it has since been restored to its proper place in the understanding of spiritual process that *Lessons in Truth* sets forth so clearly. The concern was that in telling readers about the inevitability of chemicalization, the book would be creating the experience, since we know as spiritual law that our life experience is created from the beliefs we hold in consciousness. If we believe that we will experience chemicalization, isn't it that belief that creates the experience?

Well, no. Chemicalization is an integral part of the creative process—an unwelcome by-product, perhaps, but an integral part nonetheless. That means that it is a part of divine law—the universal principles according to which the power of God expresses. Divine law exists in an infinite dimension of absolute truth that is not affected by whether we believe in it. Many people do not believe in the creative power of the beliefs we hold to be true. That doesn't mean their beliefs do not create their experiences; it simply means they are unaware of the process at work.

It's the same with chemicalization—with the Four Horsemen of Chapter 6. The process of opening the scroll is the process of creating the new consciousness that Jesus Christ describes as the kingdom of heaven. An integral part of that process involves facing and dissolving deeply-rooted fears and negative expectations that are the dark, shadowy aspects of the more limited human consciousness we are trying to release.

Chemicalization will occur whether we believe in it or not. The danger is that if we remain ignorant of its inevitability, we may well interpret these negative experiences as a sign that we're on the wrong path, and use them as an excuse to retreat from our spiritual progress. That's why, I think, the Revelation makes clear at the outset that as we allow the white-horsed Christ to ride before us and guide our journey, we can be sure that the Four Horsemen of fear-based negativity will immediately appear, eager to discourage and distract us from our new-found spiritual potential.

How powerful are they? Well—and here's the good news—that's entirely up to us. These horsemen of conflict, lack, death, retribution and chaos have no reality except what we choose to give them. Their power is simply the power of our own ignorant and misplaced faith. Their energy will dissolve as quickly—or as slowly—as we choose to reclaim that power and redirect it to the Christ that rides ahead.

So much for the notorious Four Horsemen of the Apocalypse. They are not agents of the forces of evil. They are, after all, released through the positive action of opening the seals and moving forward on our spiritual path. They represent the deeply entrenched negative beliefs on which we have been basing our choices—conflict, lack, death and divine retribution. They must be recognized and confronted before they can be dissolved. They may seem overwhelming. But before them—and before us—goes the white horse of the Christ, bringing light to the shadows and love to the fears, helping us stay firm in our commitment.

MEDITATION

I AM the Lamb of God. I AM the gentle, loving power of infinite possibility. I AM a spiritual being, here in human form to break open the seals on the scroll of spiritual truth. I understand that expressions of negative energy are an essential part of the creative process working through me. I experience them without fear or judgment, and I dissolve them easily in the light of divine love within me.

Questions for Discussion

1. What general impression did you have of the Four Horsemen of the Apocalypse before reading this chapter? Has that impression changed? How?

2. Unlike the vivid descriptions in previous chapters, we are told nothing about what these riders looked like. Why might that be?

3. In what ways do we "measure out" the good in our lives? What is the underlying belief that makes such meticulous accounting seem necessary?

4. Have you experienced negative energies as a response to positive spiritual intentions? How did you feel? What did you think? How might the experience have been different if you had been aware of the phenomenon of chemicalization?

Step 7

TAKING A BREAK

There are periodic interludes throughout the Revelation—breaks in the action that allow us to rise above the level of drama and conflict long enough to glimpse the larger view, assuring us that no matter how dark things get, we are always moving forward toward spiritual light. Chapter 7 is one of those interludes—a pause between the stormy effects of the sixth seal and the opening of the seventh.

> "After this I saw four angels standing at the four corners of the earth, holding back the four winds of the earth so that no wind could blow on earth or sea or against any tree. I saw another angel ascending from the rising of the sun, having the seal of the living God, and he called with a loud voice to the four angels who had been given power to damage earth and sea, saying, 'Do not damage the earth or the sea or the trees, until we have marked the servants of our God with a seal on their foreheads.'"

—Rev. 7:1-3

At the end of Chapter 6, everyone on earth is hiding "in the caves and among the rocks of the mountains," fearful of the terrible things that are happening. Here four angels are sent to hold back the winds—the negative energies that are about to be unleashed. And a fifth angel announces the plan: "The servants of our God" will be set apart from the general chaos, identified by a seal on their foreheads.

The forehead is the location of the pineal gland, metaphysically the "third eye" of spiritual awareness. So it would seem that those who are awake to their identity as spiritual beings, whose third eyes are able to perceive the spiritual dimension that underlies all of life, will not be buffeted about in the storms to come. This doesn't necessarily mean that they will not experience the storms; but they will not be lost and confused by them. They will understand the Spirit at work.

> "And I heard the number of those who were sealed, one hundred forty-four thousand, sealed out of every tribe of the people of Israel: From the tribe of Judah twelve thousand sealed, from the tribe of Reuben twelve thousand, from the tribe of Gad twelve thousand, from the tribe of Asher twelve thousand, from the tribe of Naphtali twelve thousand, from the tribe of Manasseh twelve thousand, from the tribe of Simeon twelve thousand, from the tribe of Levi twelve thousand, from the tribe of Issachar twelve thousand, from the tribe of Zebulun twelve thousand, from the tribe of Joseph twelve thousand, from the tribe of Benjamin twelve thousand sealed. After this I looked, and there was a great multitude that no one could count, from every nation, from all tribes and peoples and languages, standing before the throne and before the Lamb, robed in white, with palm branches in their hands."

—Rev. 7:4-9

It is a mistake to think of the numbers in the Revelation in terms of literal accuracy. As we've seen with the number seven, all numbers in scripture are emblematic of a deeper truth. Here 144,000 is 12 times 12,000; and 12 is a number of completion— the 12 tribes of Israel, the 12 apostles. We're told in Acts of the Apostles (1:21-26) that one of the first things the apostles did after Jesus left them was to elect a replacement for Judas, so that their number would still be 12. A community of 11 apostles would have been incomplete.

The promise here is that not one spiritually awake and aware individual will be excluded or overlooked. Indeed, we're told in the next sentence that the total was *a great multitude that no one could count.* They wear white robes signifying a new life, and carry palm branches of peace.

> "They cried out in a loud voice, saying, 'Salvation belongs to our God who is seated on the throne, and to the Lamb!' And all the angels stood around the throne and around the elders and the four living creatures, and they fell on their faces before the throne and worshiped God, singing, 'Amen! Blessing and glory and wisdom and thanksgiving and honor and power and might be to our God forever and ever! Amen.'"
>
> —Rev. 7:10-12

It's easy to imagine this as a massive crowd scene in a distant heaven, with the camera pulling back further and further to reveal masses of people joined in a great hymn of praise and salvation. It's more difficult—and much more important—to remember that the kingdom of God is not in a distant realm; it is within us. God is "seated on the throne" when the Christ of our own being is the focus of our faith and intention. This scene is not a part of the process; it is a vision of spiritual completion.

> "Then one of the elders addressed me, saying, 'Who are these, robed in white, and where have they come from?' I said to him, 'Sir, you are the one that knows.' Then he said to me, 'These are they who have come out of the great ordeal; they have washed their robes and made them white in the blood of the Lamb.'"
>
> —Rev. 7:13-14

There are a couple of important insights into our spiritual path contained in these few sentences. First of all, when the narrator is asked for an explanation of what he is seeing, he is spiritually wise enough to know that he doesn't know. Our experience in school leads us to believe that in order to move forward, we must understand everything; we must be able to answer every question, pass every test. Not so. Our intellect may be lost and confused. But if we have total faith in our innate oneness with Divine Mind, we can live peacefully in the question, open to the spiritual answer that will come in its proper time.

Second, it's important to note that these uncountable multitudes are not people who have been spared "the great ordeal." They have come out of it. Their white robes were once as filthy and stained with fear and negative experiences as those worn by the people still caught up in the chaos. They are not "chosen ones," special and unique. They are simply the first to awake. "The blood of the Lamb" is the life energy of Christ awareness. It will wash our tattered robes clean and fresh, and we will be "reborn" in the dimension of heaven within us.

> "For this reason they are before the throne of God, and worship him day and night within his temple, and the one who is seated on the throne will shelter them. They will hunger no more, and thirst no more; the sun will not strike them, nor any scorching heat; for the Lamb at the center of the throne will be their shepherd, and he will guide them to springs of the water of life, and God will wipe away every tear from their eyes."

—Rev. 7:15-17

We will find later echoes of this beautiful promise in the final pages of the Revelation. There are many storms and conflicts, much darkness and fear still to come. But isn't it wonderful that when we least expect it, we are granted through grace an interlude like this, assuring us that so long as we stay the course, the outcome is assured? If we continue to choose as our shepherd, through everything that is to come, the Christ Presence at the heart of our being, we will find the springs of life that Jesus promised the Samaritan woman at the well would become *"a spring of water gushing up to eternal life"* (Jn. 4:14).

Thoughts on Step 7: Taking a Break

We begin to see in this chapter, I think, how the positive and unifying message of the Revelation to John has come to be seen as just the opposite—as a message of negativity, judgment and separation. It's not simply a question of what's *in* the Revelation; it's also a question of what a reader brings *to* it.

This pause in the action before the opening of the seventh seal is clearly meant to offer a reassurance that, although our spiritual process may be chaotic, a positive, loving outcome is assured. Those who are spiritually awake to the Christ Presence within them will move the dramas of mortal life more easily and comfortably than those whose focus is entirely centered on the challenges before them. The spiritually awake will still be involved—they'll still get their hands dirty, not to mention their once-white robes. But because their focus is on the underlying spiritual process, they will find themselves centered in heaven consciousness even as the dualistic conflict unfolds.

That's what we read in the text. But it becomes something very different if we come to it with a mindset that believes in separation—specifically, in the judgmental separation of believers from nonbelievers. Actually, we're all believers at heart; even atheists *believe* there is no God. So this distinction really intends to separate "those whose beliefs agree with mine" from "those whose beliefs differ from mine."

When we approach Chapter 7 from this perspective, we can see in its imagery a justification for our eagerness to condemn others while feeling rather smug about ourselves. A God of universal love suddenly becomes a judgmental dispenser of favors. God chooses from all of creation a small, elite group of "true believers" and sets them aside for safekeeping while he lays waste to everyone else. How fortunate that we are, of course, a part of that select few! How sad that everyone whose faith differs from ours is destined for eternal perdition.

The text does not say that; but it can be *made* to say that if we come to it having already decided this is the "truth" we want to find. The text does not exclude anyone from the creative process that produces confusion and suffering. That elite 144,000 have been battered, scuffed and stained by their human adventure just as everyone else has. The message of this chapter is that once we "open our third eye" to the spiritual dimension of everything that happens, we will be able to move through the adventure without losing sight of our Oneness with divine energy.

The imagery of washing the robes would have been especially meaningful to the Revelation's intended first readers. When early followers of Jesus chose to become members of the spiritual community focused on his teachings, they went through a sacrament of baptism. They removed their clothing and walked into a body of water for full immersion. As they emerged, they were dressed in a white robe signifying a new beginning. Now, aware of themselves as the Christ—"Christ in you, the hope of glory" as Paul put it in his letter to the Colossians (1:27)—their lives truly began anew. They would still experience the challenges of their humanity—indeed, those challenges might well increase because of their new commitment—but they would understand that everything was in furtherance of our innate spiritual purpose, which was then and is now the creation of the new consciousness that is the kingdom of heaven.

It's sad, I think, that the phrase "born again" has come to be associated exclusively with the fundamentalist view that our only job is to "accept Jesus Christ as our Lord and Savior." That's important, of course; we "accept" Jesus when we believe in his teachings and follow his example. We may with equal spiritual awareness "accept" the Buddha when we believe in his expressions of the same principles, and follow the example of his life—or that of Muhammad, or Confucius or any other spiritual guide.

But being born again is not just a matter of deciding to trust in one spiritual teacher or another. It requires us to trust equally in ourselves, having faith in our own Christ nature as we set out to transform the world as he did. Being born again is not about separating ourselves contentedly from the rest of humankind. It's about embracing our Oneness with all of creation, and the infinite Light and Love that is expressing in all of it—and through all of us.

MEDITATION

I AM centered in my innate Christ nature. I move through every challenge, and dissolve every negative thought, in quiet confidence. In embracing my spiritual purpose, I AM truly reborn.

Questions for Discussion

1. Your interest in the Revelation to John suggests that you have had your own sense of spiritual awakening. What happened? How did you change as a result?

2. Why do you think we share a tendency to judge other beliefs negatively if they differ from our own? Is it because we are so sure that we are right? Or is there an underlying fear that we might be wrong?

3. What does Paul's phrase "hope of glory" suggest to you? How might that hope express in your life today?

4. How might we serve the Power of God "day and night within his temple"? How do you understand the promises that conclude this chapter?

Step 8

TRUMPETING CHAOS

After the interlude of Chapter 7, we return to the drama at hand: the opening of the seven seals on the scroll of life. Six have already been opened, releasing first the power of the Christ, which goes before us, and then the horsemen representing the major challenges we will be facing on our spiritual path: war, famine, pestilence and death. The opening of the sixth seal released negative energies sufficient to engender a profound fear in the hearts of "the rich and the powerful, and every one, slave and free" (6:15).

Now, having been reassured that a positive outcome is guaranteed, it is time to open the seventh seal.

> "When the Lamb opened the seventh seal, there was silence in heaven for about half an hour. And I saw the seven angels who stand before God, and seven trumpets were given to them."
>
> —Rev. 8:1-2

I really like the half hour of silence. I have seen expressions of it many times in my own life. I may know that a climactic moment is at hand. All hell (literally) is about to break loose. I brace myself for the storm—and, indeed, a storm will appear. But first, this little grace note of "silence in heaven for about half an hour." It's calming. It allows me time to breathe, to remember that the storms to come are not the sum total of my existence. They are simply a part of my spiritual purpose. And in the infinite, unexpressed energy of God that fills the silence lies all the power and love I will need to move through, and move on.

> "Another angel with a golden censer came and stood at the altar; he was given a great quantity of incense to offer with the prayers of all the saints on the golden altar that is before the throne. And the smoke of the incense, with the prayers of the saints, rose before God from the hand of the angel. Then the angel took the censer and filled it with fire from the altar and threw it on the earth; and there were peals of thunder, rumblings, flashes of lightning, and an earthquake."
>
> —Rev. 8:3-5

This image would have evoked in its earliest readers memories of the Temple in Jerusalem and the deeply meaningful rituals that had long been performed there. For us, reading it today, it serves as a strong reminder that all the drama about to unfold on Earth—thunder, lightning, earthquake—have their source in the realm of Spirit. They are not the punishment of an angry God; they are a response to our prayers! We have made a commitment to accept and pursue the spiritual purpose that brought us into this human experience. That commitment calls us to embark upon a path that—as Jesus taught repeatedly—is not for the faint of heart.

> "Now the seven angels who had the seven trumpets made ready to blow them."
>
> —Rev. 8:6

I think it's worth pausing for a moment to appreciate the skill and underlying structure that have gone into the author's efforts to express his visions in terms we can clearly grasp. The seventh seal brings seven angels with seven trumpets—it's almost like a fairy tale, or a Mother Goose rhyme. "When I was going to St. Ives, I met a man with seven wives. And every wife had seven cats ..." But I digress.

The drama about to unfold will require our full spiritual commitment. Anything less will find us stuck in the illusion instead of moving through to the positive outcome promised at the end of the last chapter. That's why so much of the vision's early energy is devoted to awakening those seven spiritual centers within us—the churches, the chakras, the energy that can only be released if we allow the Lamb, the Christ, to open our seven seals. Now we're about to learn just why we need all of that energy.

> "The first angel blew his trumpet, and there came hail and fire, mixed with blood, and they were hurled to the earth; and a third of the earth was burned up, and a third of the trees were burned up, and all green grass was burned up."
>
> —Rev. 8:7

The consequences released by the seven angels are similar to the plagues inflicted on Egypt in the Book of Exodus (Chapters 7-10). In that case and this, the underlying message is the same: Choices have consequences. If we choose to keep our spiritual energies enslaved to human values, as the Pharaoh was determined to do, there will be painful negative consequences. Also, if we commit to moving further on our spiritual path, the first necessity will be to experience and release the consequences that have accumulated from fear-based choices we've made in the past. Hail is ice, of course, so we are experiencing an assault of opposites—ice and fire—mixed with the blood energy of our long-held beliefs in the dualistic challenge they represent.

> "The second angel blew his trumpet, and something like a great mountain, burning with fire, was thrown

into the sea. A third of the sea became blood, a third
of the living creatures in the sea died, and a third of the
ships were destroyed."

—Rev. 8:8

There are two common themes in the consequences of the
first four trumpet blasts described in this chapter. The first is
the presence of fire as a force of both destruction and purification. The second is the consistent promise that the destruction
is limited to one-third of the expressions of life on the planet.
That's a lot, but it could be much worse. What is destroyed in
this spiritual process are expressions derived from completely
false belief—belief in the reality of separation, lack and limitation. It may seem at times that everything we experience is a
creation of false belief, but that is not so. Many of our thoughts
and choices—two-thirds, according to this vision—are viable,
but imperfect, expressions of spiritual Truth. They are the fish
Jesus describes (Mt. 13:47-50) as being worthy of accompanying
us into the kingdom of heaven. They are purified by the same
fire that destroys the false.

Note how the order of destruction and purification described
here follows the first order of creation described in Genesis
(1:1-2:3). We are precisely following the creative process of the
divine as we allow its infinite energy to move through us.

"The third angel blew his trumpet, and a great star fell
from heaven, blazing like a torch, and it fell on a third
of the rivers and on the springs of water. The name of
the star is Wormwood. A third of the waters became
wormwood, and many died from the water, because it
was made bitter.

The fourth angel blew his trumpet, and a third of the
sun was struck, and a third of the moon, and a third
of the stars, so that a third of their light was darkened;

a third of the day was kept from shining, and likewise the night."

—Rev. 8:10-12

Each day of creation in Genesis ends with the statement "God saw that it was good." That "good" is still everywhere present, because God is everywhere present. Humankind, as a consequence of forgetting our spiritual identity and spiritual mission, has mis-created expressions of fear thoughts. It is probably easier today than it has ever been to recognize the ways in which our fear-based energies of greed and exploitation have negatively impacted the very planet that is our mortal home. Even that recognition, however, tempts us to affirm duality by blaming others and making ourselves victims. It is only by allowing the power of heaven, "blazing like a torch" within us, to literally change our minds that we will be able to recreate and reclaim the eternal good of the initial creation.

"Then I looked, and I heard an eagle crying with a loud voice as it flew in mid-heaven, 'Woe, woe, woe to the inhabitants of the earth, at the blasts of the other trumpets that the three angels are about to blow!'"

—Rev. 8:13

"Woe, woe, woe"—one for each angel still to come—is both a warning that the process is not yet complete, and an expression of loving sympathy for those of us who are embracing the process and experiencing the pain of its early stages.

Thoughts on Step 8: Trumpeting Chaos

It is something of a New Thought cliché to affirm that "religion" is for people who are afraid of going to hell, and "spirituality" is for people who have already been there. Like every cliché, it's an unsupportable generality that nonetheless contains a germ of significant truth.

Many people turn to religion in the belief—or at least hope—that it will offer them a way out of the pains and challenges of this human experience. Central to this dimension of faith is the understanding that we have "fallen" from a state of pure bliss as a consequence of an act of disobedience immediately after our creation. This fall-based understanding of the human condition tells us that all the negative energies we label as suffering are a result of that disobedience—and of our continuing refusal to live in perfect obedience to the dictates of the Creator, a being named God.

Does that describe the underlying religious understanding in which you were raised? For most of us, I think it does. Whether our families were particularly religious, it's an understanding that colors our entire culture—our churches, of course, but also our schools, media, politics. Humankind is inherently flawed. It is because of that flaw that we experience challenge and suffering in our lives. There is a better place—in fact, a perfect place—where we once were, and still could be, but we blew it. We're here to experience the absence of God, and to entreat God to grant us loving favors we don't really deserve. Ultimately, the only real hope is that we will be rewarded for our obedience after we die, by being allowed entrance to a better place. In addition, if our obedience is insufficient, we will be condemned by our own Creator to spend all eternity in a place of constant pain and suffering, a place from which God is eternally absent.

Please note that there is significant spiritual truth in that construct. Suffering is, indeed, a consequence of our own choices—not because God is punishing us, but because we are punishing ourselves. Obedience to divine law is, indeed, the appropriate path through the human experience—not because we are judged and graded according to our submissiveness, but because divine law offers the one true guide to fulfilling our creative purpose. There is, indeed, a more perfect life experience available to us—not in a different location after we die, but in our own consciousness here and now, as we surrender our belief in separation and embrace the spiritual truth that we are, now and always, one with the energy of perfect love and infinite creative empowerment that is God.

And yes, "hell" is indeed the experience of the absence of God, and it hurts like—well, you know. But let's think for just a moment. We universally affirm that God is an energy of omniscience, omnipotence and omnipresence. Take away those qualities—deny God the three *omnis*—and you have a limited God. But that is neither our belief nor our experience.

If there is a place called "hell" that is defined as someplace where God is absent, then we don't have an omnipresent God. Similarly, if we seriously believe there is a power *opposite* to God whose sworn purpose is to undo all that God is and does, then we don't have an omnipotent God.

No, we can't limit God. But we can certainly limit our understanding of God. There can't be an actual place in which God is absent. But we can choose to experience the illusion of God's absence. And that's what we do, out of ignorance or fear, when we choose to believe in a distant, judgmental God from which we are separated by a gulf of guilt and shame.

When we are fully committed to our innate oneness with the divine, and in the process of expressing our spiritual purpose, "hell" isn't a future possibility—it's a past experience. We come from a hell of our own making, a sense of separation and isolation so complete the pain becomes unendurable. We begin to move out of that hell the moment we surrender to the truth of our eternal oneness with everything God is.

The journey out of hell is fraught with challenges but—here's the good news—there's no going back. Oh, we can try. Feeling sorry for ourselves as victims condemned to hell sometimes has its appeal to our nutty human minds. But there's no going back. They say about Alcoholics Anonymous that, whether you stick with it or not, it really screws up your drinking. What that means is that we can choose to return to hell, but we can never again believe that we have no choice. We can't believe ourselves to be victims of forces beyond our control. And sooner or later, knowing our residence in hell is a choice we are making, we're going to decide to leave. When? That's entirely up to us.

MEDITATION

I center myself, many times each day, in the "silence in heaven" I find at the heart of my being. In that silence of perfect peace, I see all the events of my life as opportunities to express my true Christ identity.

Questions for Discussion

1. Have you experienced "silence in heaven" at key moments in your life? What was that like? What was the result?

2. Tell of an experience in your life that initially seemed to be completely negative, but that resulted in a significant blessing. What lesson did you learn as a result?

3. Rev. Ed's favorite prayer is just four words: *Show me the good*. How does that pertain to the actions of the four angels in this chapter?

4. Have you been to hell? What was it like? How did you know you were there? What prompted you to leave?

Step 9

ENDURING THREE PLAGUES

The overall effect of Chapter 9 will depend a lot on how you feel about locusts. We are continuing to experience the effects of the trumpets—the "noise" we make when we begin to awaken to our spiritual purpose. Like hearing a loud alarm clock in the early morning, our initial response may be anger, fear and confusion. We've become so familiar to the "dream" of duality that anything else seems threatening. But if we take the time to center ourselves in our own Christ energy, even the most voracious locusts won't disturb us.

> "And the fifth angel blew his trumpet, and I saw a star that had fallen from heaven to earth, and he was given the key to the shaft of the bottomless pit; he opened the shaft of the bottomless pit, and from the shaft rose smoke like the smoke of a great furnace, and the sun and the air were darkened with the smoke from the shaft."
>
> —Rev. 9:1-2

We've already agreed that a bottomless pit must, by very definition, be an illusion. If it's an illusion, then it's of our own making. So this fifth trumpet—symbolizing the throat chakra, the center of spiritual power—is the key that allows us to open the illusive pit, releasing its dark smoke so it can be dissolved in *the sun and the air*. The initial effect may be alarmingly dark and sooty, but the clearing that results is a great benefit as our journey continues.

"Then from the smoke came locusts on the earth, and they were given authority like the authority of scorpions of the earth. They were told not to damage the grass of the earth or any green growth or any tree, but only those people who do not have the seal of God on their foreheads. They were allowed to torture them for five months, but not to kill them, and their torture was like the torture of a scorpion when it stings someone. And in those days people will seek death but will not find it; they will long to die, but death will flee from them."

—Rev. 9:3-6

Again we have an apparently deliberate echo of the plagues described in Exodus. The significant difference is that the Egyptian locusts are meant to be totally destructive; they "shall eat every tree of yours which grows in the field, and they shall fill your houses" (Ex. 10:5). Here they are carefully limited in what they are sent to do. Nothing is to be destroyed, or even damaged; those who have not yet awakened to the spiritual dimension of the unfolding drama are to be stung—painfully, but not fatally—for a limited period of time.

The fact that death was not to be a factor would seem to be good news. But, in fact, death is the ultimate escape fantasy. It's the darkest illusion of separation and limitation we can devise. That's why Jesus decided to make his departure from human form a powerful demonstration of the eternal life that is our truth, hoping that we would thereby release our addiction to the finality and hopelessness of death. For those still living with false beliefs, death is the vindication that justifies those beliefs. That's why it is lovingly withheld—death is an illusory cop-out that has no place in our spiritual progress.

"In appearance the locusts were like horses equipped for battle. On their heads were what looked like crowns of gold; their faces were like human faces, their hair like women's hair, and their teeth like lions' teeth; they had scales like iron breastplates, and the noise of their wings was like the noise of many chariots with horses rushing into battle. They have tails like scorpions, with stingers, and in their tails is their power to harm people for five months. They have as king over them the angel of the bottomless pit; his name in Hebrew is Abaddon, and in Greek he is called Apollyon."

—Rev. 9:7-11

These are clearly not your everyday locusts. They are painstakingly described, and the overall effect is one of conflict and deception. They come, remember, from the bottomless pit—the realm of shadows and negative energy in which we hide our darkest fears. They are scary, but their power is limited; the only requirement for dealing with them is not the courage to fight them—that would simply empower their warlike energy—but the patience to wait them out.

Who is in charge of these locusts, these false gods with human faces and angry attributes? "In Hebrew he is Abaddon, and in Greek he is called Apollyon." Both names translate as "Destroyer." Interesting, no? In Hindu mythology, the god of destruction is Shiva, and his skill is understood to be an essential element in the cycle of life. The old must be destroyed in order for the new to express, so Shiva is welcomed as an avatar of the creative process. Destruction may be painful but, as with these locusts, the pain is temporary, and the benefit is eternal.

"The first woe has passed. There are still two woes to come.

> Then the sixth angel blew his trumpet, and I heard a voice from the four horns of the golden altar before God, saying to the sixth angel who had the trumpet, 'Release the four angels who are bound at the great river Euphrates.' So the four angels were released, who had been held ready for the hour, the day, the month, and the year, to kill a third of humankind. The number of the troops of cavalry was two hundred million; I heard their number."

—Rev. 9:12-16

The Euphrates River was the Eastern boundary of the Roman Empire, essentially the end of the civilized world. Little was known about the Parthians who lived beyond the Euphrates; and ignorance, of course, breeds fear and rumor. In folklore and legends of the time, Parthians played approximately the role that men from Mars played in 1950s science fiction; they symbolized the unknown.

We have fears in consciousness that correspond to these cavalrymen. We have created comfort zones for ourselves—areas of belief, tradition and habit consisting of thoughts, feelings and information that have always worked well for us. Outside this comfort zone lurk those thoughts, feelings and ideas that seem alien to us. We don't want to deal with them, or even to acknowledge their presence in the farther reaches of consciousness. But the more we try to ignore this cavalry of unnamed fears, the more power we give them. It's time to take a stand, and see just what it is we're so afraid of.

> "And this was how I saw the horses in my vision: the riders wore breastplates the color of fire and of sapphire and of sulfur; the heads of the horses were like lions' heads, and fire and smoke and sulfur came out of their mouths. By these three plagues a third of humankind was killed, by the fire and smoke and sulfur coming out

of their mouths. For the power of the horses is in their mouths and in their tails; their tails are like serpents, having heads; and with them they inflict harm."

—Rev. 9:17-19

It sounds silly, I suppose, but what this image most reminds me of is the experience of giving up cigarettes. In their absence, I was made painfully aware of what my smoking addiction had meant. The danger of fire, the obscuring quality of smoke, and the noxious smell of sulfur offer a perfect description of the way in which I used cigarettes to keep fears, doubts—and other people—at bay, to protect my personal comfort zone, my sense of self. Here our willingness to engage in this chaotic creative process forces us to allow the cavalry to dissolve the negative thoughts that would serve to hold us back. It may feel like we are being destroyed in the process; but only the dark, shadow thoughts are being released. There is twice as much light as darkness within us on even our darkest days.

"The rest of humankind, who were not killed by these plagues, did not repent of the works of their hands or give up worshiping demons and idols of gold and silver and bronze and stone and wood, which cannot see or hear or walk. And they did not repent of their murders or their sorceries or their fornication or their thefts."

—Rev. 9:20-21

We aren't "there" yet, wherever "there" may ultimately prove to be. It's tempting every time we take a step forward—as we have done here by releasing the cavalry—to believe that the challenge is over, the journey is complete. But we have managed to deeply entrench ourselves in an energy of illusion and ignorance concerning our true identity and purpose. Making the things of this world—especially *idols of gold and silver*—more important than our spiritual purpose is the ultimate addiction.

We have become addicted to our humanness, addicted to being victims of forces beyond our control. There are more challenges to be faced, more new choices to be made, before we are fully the Christ in expression we must be to create the new kingdom consciousness. And, of course, it is only out of that new consciousness that the kingdom itself will come.

Thoughts on Step 9: Enduring Three Plagues

In discussing the Revelation to John in classes and workshops over the past few years, by far the most frequently asked questions have been, "How do you know? How do you know what all these images mean? How do you know that it describes a positive spiritual process rather than a negative religious judgment?"

These are important questions, of course. And since the symbols are beginning to come thick and fast, this might be a good time to address it.

The quick answer is, I don't know. At least, I can't offer any absolute proof that would be acceptable to an inherently doubting, scientific mindset. No archeologist on Patmos has unearthed a glossary of terms that John used 2,000 years ago in describing what were, to him, highly disturbing visions. How, then, are we to understand those visions today? And—to cut to the chase here—why bother?

Let's begin by recognizing the three dimensions at which the Bible—or any Scripture—expresses. The first is the dimension of history. Each individual work that became a part of the canonical Bible was written by a specific person (or persons) at a specific time. The Hebrew Scriptures that make up the Christian Old Testament are the history of the Hebrew people from their beginnings as a nomadic tribe through the establishment of the kingdom of Israel and the sequential conquering and occupation of that nation by the forces of Babylon, Greece and Rome. The New Testament is the history of what came to be the Christian Church, from the life of its central teacher through its tentative early days as an offshoot of Judaism to its establishment as a religious force throughout the Roman Empire. More than just a factual account, at this level the Bible includes the stories, songs, poems and other writings that were important to the Judeo-Christian culture as its history unfolded. The question asked and answered is, What happened?

At the second level, the relevant question might be, Why did it happen? More to the point, What does the information tell us about how to live mortal lives in obedience to divine law? The great Unity Bible teacher Rev. Frank Giudici, whose enthusiasm proved to be so amazingly contagious, used to sum up the central theme of the entire Bible in three simple words: "Put God First!" The events of history happened, from this perspective, because the people either did or did not put God first. The writings all describe how well things will go if you do, and how terribly painful things can become if you don't. Obedience to the laws of God is the overt concern of this second level.

These two dimensions—the historic and the religious—represent the way in which most of us were first introduced to the Bible—and it is in reaction to these two levels that many people accept it, and others reject it. I, for one, had no interest in the Bible at these levels. It seemed terribly dated and of questionable accuracy. Rituals, traditions, beliefs and superstitions from thousands of years ago had no apparent relevance to modern life. It contained practices—animal sacrifice, slavery, the subjugation of women for example—that were no longer considered divinely sanctioned. So if some parts of it had to be disregarded, why should I bother paying attention to the rest?

This was my general attitude at about the time Unity entered my life and opened the door to a third layer of meaning and message—and slowly the Bible became a fascinating, living, breathing support system for a spiritual journey that I barely understood. The spiritual catalyst was the work of Charles Fillmore in approaching the Bible as a sort of metaphysical road map to our own collective spiritual unfoldment.

This metaphysical approach does not deny or invalidate the levels of history and morality. It simply goes deeper. It recognizes that true scripture is an expression of divine energy. It cannot age or become dated. There is something eternally true at its heart.

We've seen that the relevant questions at the first two levels are, What happened? And why did it happen? The metaphysical question is this: How does this happen in me? Metaphysically, the Bible is both the story of our collective expansion in consciousness as we work to fulfill our spiritual purpose within this human illusion, and the story of how that same expansion expresses in each of us individually.

At this level, all the characters who appear and disappear, fight and love, remember God and forget God, make woeful mistakes and accomplish great things, represent thoughts in our own minds—individually and collectively. Metaphysically, the Bible—from the first words of Genesis to the final words of this Revelation to John—describes how we, created as eternal spiritual beings, move into the density of this human experience and begin to believe in its limitations, fears and judgments, forgetting in the process that we, as beings of spirit, are powerful over it all. It then describes the struggle to remember and reclaim our spiritual truth, to affirm and express the Christ that we truly are so that, choice by choice, we transform this illusion of limitation into the experience of light, love and joy that is the kingdom of heaven.

Suddenly, with this understanding, the Bible ceases to be a fusty artifact from the past. It's as immediate as this morning's *New York Times*, and a lot more honest and helpful about the spiritual guidance that will move each of us individually through challenges and on to new possibilities.

Now the Revelation to John has little or nothing to say about the first two levels of Bible approach. All we know about what's happening is that some guy named John on an island named Patmos is writing about some visions. True, there are mysterious references to events of the day, but no useful information.

Who was this John? Was he a loving spiritual teacher or a cranky nutcase? Did he do something to deserve these visions? Or was he chosen at random? We don't know. So the "why" of the second level doesn't come into play at all.

Yet here it is—the final bookend to the amazing collection of writings we call the Bible. There must be a reason—and there is. When we approach the Revelation metaphysically, we find a clear, vivid, scary but ultimately loving description of the same spiritual process on which the entire Bible has been focused.

And herein lies the answer to the question I started with. If the Revelation to John is divinely inspired to speak directly to you about your own spiritual journey, then you are the only one who can know what it means—for you! The most I can do is point out some of the ways in which these visions do, in fact, express the universal principles that are intended to guide that journey.

After all, the Revelation doesn't stand alone. It cannot have a message that runs counter to the entire rest of the Bible. The realization of God as a power of infinite love cannot become an experience of God as a limited, vindictive creator willing to condemn his own creation to eternal damnation.

Many people shun the Revelation to John precisely because they are afraid of what they've been taught is its message of doom and eternal suffering. But that cannot be its message if it is truly a work of scripture. It's a message of hope and love. It doesn't flinch from the fact that the process can seem truly frightening, that we will have to deal with illusions of anger, hatred and judgment. Our mortal mind will not let go gracefully; it will do everything it can to prevent us from reaching that spring of eternal life. However, the final work of the Bible cannot have as its purpose persuading us to believe the negative illusions. It's one final, triumphant invitation to move fearlessly past the illusions of darkness into the truth of spiritual light.

I have referred earlier to an approach to the Bible known as *maieutic*, from the Greek word for "midwife." Its basic premise is that it is not the teacher's job to impart information to a student. It is rather the teacher's job to help the students give birth to what is already within them. We are all one with Divine Mind; we already have access to all knowing. You already know what the Revelation means to you. My job—my hope—is to make some suggestions that might help you give birth to that meaning.

So if my understanding of something doesn't work for you—great! What exactly doesn't feel right about it? What would feel more appropriate to you? So long as we agree that scripture cannot violate the universal spiritual principles that govern our relationship to the divine, we have total freedom in understanding how those principles are expressing through the Revelation.

MEDITATION

I AM calm and centered as I face the locusts of fear-based thoughts and the armies of negative energies that are released in consciousness by my willingness to be the Christ in full expression. I dissolve them in the light of spiritual love and guidance, and I joyfully continue my journey.

Questions for Discussion

1. What do the specific attributes of the locusts suggest to you?
2. If the locusts represent repressed consequences of choices made in our former, fear-based consciousness, what names might some of these locusts have for you?
3. This "first woe" passes without any effort on our part except to unlock the bottomless pit. We don't have to destroy the locusts—they simply lose power after a period of time. What does this suggest?
4. How do "fire, smoke and sulfur" express in our lives today? How do they discourage us from continuing on our spiritual path?

Step 10

RENEWING OUR PURPOSE

C hapter 10 offers another interlude in the unfolding dra-ma—a "time-out" after the plague of locusts. I think this rhythm of action and rest is more than a literary convention. It offers one of the Revelation's most important messages. Just as a seventh day of rest is an essential part of the creative process described in Genesis, so, too, is it essential that we allow periods of rest in the journey we have undertaken to realize our spiritual purpose. There is no hurry. There can't be because there is no time in the dimension of spirit. Time is strictly a factor of the human illusion, and we are releasing the power of the illusion in order to claim our truth. So we appreciate these interludes as reminders of the bigger picture, and we trust the rhythm of God to move us forward.

> "And I saw another mighty angel coming down from heaven, wrapped in a cloud, with a rainbow over his head; his face was like the sun, and his legs like pillars of fire. He held a little scroll open in his hand. Setting his right foot on the sea and his left foot on the land, he gave a great shout, like a lion roaring. And when he shouted, the seven thunders sounded. And when the seven thunders had sounded, I was about to write, but I heard a voice from heaven saying, 'Seal up what the seven thunders have said, and do not write it down.'"

—Rev. 10:1-4

We know this angel brings good news because he comes with a rainbow—the symbol of the covenant between God and mankind described in the story of Noah (Genesis, Chapters 6-9). In that covenant, God promises not to destroy the creation, and mankind agrees to follow the guidance of divine law as it moves through the human experience. Angels are metaphysical representations of that guidance—messages from Divine Mind expressing in our consciousness—and this particular guidance is both large and loud.

Rainbows, containing as they do a full spectrum of color, represent divine love, creativity and infinite possibility. So this oversized angel is not meant to be frightening, but powerful. He delivers a ringing wake-up call that contains our personal, unique spiritual mission. It need not be written down, because it's meant for us alone. Each of us will hear our own thundering angel, carrying a little scroll on which is recorded the spiritual commitment we made before entering into this particular human experience.

Each one of us is like a unique piece of an infinite jigsaw puzzle. The finished puzzle will depict the kingdom of heaven, and every piece is essential if the puzzle is to be completely assembled. The rules of assembly are the same for all of us, but finding where our individual pieces belong requires personal guidance as well. We've been occupied so far largely with the universal laws of assembly, represented by the large scroll with seven seals we encountered in Chapter 5. Now it's time to begin to explore our individual paths to find where our contributions are meant to express.

"Then the angel whom I saw standing on the sea and the land raised his right hand to heaven and swore by him who lives forever and ever, who created heaven and what is in it, the earth and what is in it, and the sea and what is in it: 'There will be no more delay, but in the days when the seventh angel is to blow his trumpet, the mystery of God will be fulfilled, as he announced to his servants the prophets.'"

—Rev. 10:5-7

Coming as it does as an interlude of calm after we have had to deal with all the locusts of our old consciousness, this is a strong reassurance that we're on the right path. Again, seven is the number of spiritual completion, and the assurance here is that completion lies just ahead on the path we're traveling. We may not understand what's happening—did we really need those locusts?—or why we need to be making this journey in the first place. That's okay. "The mystery of God will be fulfilled" when we are fully expressive of our Christ identity. And that's the "completion" that calls us forward.

"Then the voice that I had heard from heaven spoke to me again, saying, 'Go, take the scroll that is open in the hand of the angel who is standing on the sea and on the land.' So I went to the angel and told him to give me the little scroll; and he said to me, 'Take it, and eat; it will be bitter to your stomach, but sweet as honey in your mouth.' So I took the little scroll from the hand of the angel and ate it; it was sweet as honey in my mouth, but when I had eaten it, my stomach was made bitter."

—Rev. 10:8-10

Every time I read this passage, I am reminded of Robert Heinlein's sci-fi classic *Stranger in a Strange Land*—particularly his invention of the word *grok* to describe a deep process of not simply learning or observing something, but of completely ingesting it so you become totally one with it. It's a word the author made up, but it has attained such wide usage that it can be found in the *Oxford English Dictionary*. I think that's because no other word quite describes the process in which the observer and the observed become one. That's what happens here with the little scroll of personal spiritual empowerment. It's not to be shared with the world, and it's not enough to simply study it. It must be *grokked*.

Nothing can be sweeter than the discovery that we each have a unique and important spiritual purpose and identity. It gives meaning to everything. It also commits us to a Hero's Journey that will be dark, discouraging and challenging in many ways. The sweetness is a promise; the bitterness is a warning of shadows still to come.

> "Then they said to me, 'You must prophesy again about many peoples and nations and languages and kings.'"
> —Rev. 10:11

It is tempting to become so comfortable in one of these interludes—these assurances of ultimate success—that we decide to stop where we are. The locusts are gone, nothing else is threatening at the moment, and the calm feels nice. Maybe it's not the kingdom, but it's better than where we've been.

The late Unity minister Jack Boland liked to say the good is the enemy of the best. Compared to what we've been through, "good" feels pretty comfortable. It's not "best," but it's good enough. The temptation is strong to settle in.

Perhaps that's why it's not just one angel but many— "they"—who join together to nudge us out of this comfort zone and back onto the path. It's not enough to simply lift our own consciousness to a higher plane. There are "peoples and nations and languages and kings" still locked in victim consciousness. They are our work to do. So it's time to move on.

Thoughts on Step 10: Renewing Our Purpose

This welcome interlude offers a good opportunity to take a longer view of the spiritual process in which we are engaged. Particularly, it allows us to appreciate the description of that process known as the Hero's Journey. What is it? How can understanding more about it help as we venture forward?

The man most associated with the idea of the Hero's Journey is the late mythologist and teacher Joseph Campbell. In his numerous books—particularly *The Hero With a Thousand Faces*—and in a popular series of PBS interviews with Bill Moyers, Campbell shared his fascination with the common elements he saw in the great myths and legends from every culture on the planet. Characters, settings and other elements varied widely; but at heart, all of mythology seems to be telling the same story. Campbell called this story the Hero's Journey, and he worked tirelessly until his death in 1987 defining and studying this shared story.

Myths and legends might be defined as stories with no definable author; they seem to emerge from the collective subconscious, passed on orally for many generations, with each storyteller adding details and embellishments. I believe the same universal elements can also express through a single author, if he or she writes in a state of complete surrender to the creative power of the divine. This is why certain books have nearly become universal myths themselves. *The Wizard of Oz* is one classic example. Thanks both to L. Frank Baum's original book—still in print after more than a century—and the classic 1939 film version, the story, characters and even some classic lines are recognized today throughout the world. I think the seven *Harry Potter* novels by J.K. Rowling qualify as well. These stories—and many others we love to read and reread and share with our children—conform to the structure of the Hero's Journey—not because their authors deliberately chose it, but because in all the variations of that structure, we find the one true and important story of every human life.

There are many ways of analyze the Hero's Journey and many defining qualities. One is that every such journey ends where it begins. Dorothy Gale's adventure begins and ends in Kansas. Each of Harry Potter's yearlong adventures at Hogwarts begins and ends on Privet Lane. Alice, for all her Wonderland adventures, must return to her comfortable English home.

This circular construct helps us to see that we may be engaged in many different Hero's Journeys at the same time. There is the journey of a lifetime, which we begin and end in the realm of spirit. There are many journeys within one lifetime—childhood, college, employment, marriage, parenthood. In fact, every day can be seen as a distinct Hero's Journey, which we begin and end in the restful ease of sleep.

In every such journey, no matter how long or brief it may be, it is not the world around us that changes. Harry Potter's Privet Lane is as stultifying as ever each time he returns. Kansas is the same colorless environment when Dorothy finds her way back as it had been before the tornado carried her away; it is totally unaffected by her colorful Oz adventures.

No, the crucial change that is the purpose of every Hero's Journey is entirely an inside job. *We* change; and we then *become* the change we had previously demanded of the world. We find that we are different in relationship to our surroundings, which may—or may not—cause others in the world around us to change as well.

It must be obvious by now that, to me, the Hero's Journey is simply the universal way we define and describe our individual and collective spiritual process. So the Revelation to John is, at heart, a Hero's Journey in which the narrator/visionary is taken on a journey through the challenges of and promises of that process. It's a story that ends where it begins—in the Allness that is God. Nothing changes in that Allness, but we change in our relationship to it.

One of my favorite ways of working with the Hero's Journey is by appreciating the five roles—the great psychiatrist Karl Jung called them *archetypes*—we move through in the course of the journey. The first is Orphan. It is often literally true that the protagonist is an orphan—Dorothy Gale, Luke Skywalker, Harry Potter, Frodo Baggins. Even if there are parents around somewhere, there is nonetheless a sense of not belonging, a restless sense that this familial comfort zone is not really our home.

There is always an "unusual occurrence" that urges us to act on that restlessness—an owl with an invitation, a droid with news of a princess in distress, a white rabbit with a pocket watch. Something urges us forward, and we next assume the archetype of the Wanderer. We don't know anything, really. We don't know where we are or where we're going. We may have an objective in mind—rescue the princess, learn the art of wizardry, maybe simply find our way back to Kansas. But we are clueless as to the real purpose of the journey and its lessons.

We may be a Wanderer for quite a long time. It took 40 years for the Hebrew people in the wilderness to complete a journey that should have taken a fraction of that time. It's possible to become quite comfortable with wandering—packing up and moving out whenever we choose.

Meanwhile, the fact we're on the move has alarmed those thoughts in consciousness that fervently believe in the rules and limitations of the comfort zone we left and are frightened by our new boldness. This gives rise to the third archetype—the Victim. We're now at the opposite end of the circle from our beginning point, and we seem to be dealing with nothing but shadows. We may be imprisoned or in hiding. Everyone and everything seems to be against us. We can't trust anyone, and it seems clear that leaving home was a terrible mistake.

Sooner or later, we grow tired of living like this, shrinking from every shadow, and we decide to take a stand. We become the Warrior. As we move forward, we are astonished to find we have more power than we had ever imagined. The dualistic illusions from which we had been so fearfully running simply dissolve in the light of our new commitment.

This leads to the fifth and final role, that of the Wizard. This is often described as the Master of Two Worlds. Think of the traditional tarot image of the Magician, with one arm raised to heaven and the other pointing to symbols of this mortal realm. We are now centered in spiritual truth, which allows us to bring that truth into the human illusion. It is as the Wizard that we close the circle, returning to our starting point, able to enrich those aspects of it that once made us restless.

Then, one day, the restlessness will begin again, and we will know we're being called to another journey. But we won't be traveling the same circle. We'll be spiraling upward, achieving a still-higher dimension of unity. The roles will be the same, but they won't surprise us now. We won't despair; we'll keep moving. We'll encourage others who may be on their first journey. We'll learn from masters who have completed many circles. We won't be traveling for our personal good so much as we will be serving the collective consciousness.

I see the Bible as the ultimate Hero's Journey—from the Adam consciousness of early Genesis to the Christ Consciousness we've already seen in the Revelation to John, riding on ahead, to greet us further up the path. In a sense, the Revelation is like an intense refresher course—a microcosmic reminder of where we've been and where we're going. It will be good, I think, to keep the universally recognized elements of the journey in mind as we approach the shadows and scary illusions of the central chapters.

MEDITATION

I AM a spiritual hero, committed to a great creative purpose. Every choice, every challenge, every encounter in my life has a depth of meaning and significance beyond my human understanding. I trust the guidance of the Christ within me, and I move forward in confidence and love.

Questions for Discussion

1. What do you think "the seven thunders" said, and why are we not to write it down? Do you think we sometimes prefer to deal with loud, noisy dramas about the fate of the world instead of the smaller challenges we can actually do something about?

2. What do you think your little scroll says? How do you "eat" the scroll? Can you think of an example from your own life?

3. It's been said that the role of the prophet is to comfort the afflicted, and to afflict the comfortable. How does sharing spiritual truth accomplish both goals? Why should the comfortable be afflicted? Can that be done with love?

4. Think of a Hero's Journey on which you are currently engaged. It may be the journey of your entire life or of some specific part. Which of the five archetypes seems to describe where you are now? What would it take to move you to the next?

Step 11

SENSING THINGS TO COME

It feels like the journey begins in earnest with Step 11. So far, we've been going through a process of preparation, without really knowing what we're preparing *for*. The quiet interlude of Step 10 gave us a better idea of what might lie ahead. We are to "prophesy about many peoples and nations and tongues and kings," and as we do, we will be arousing resistance wherever we turn. We can understand this information in terms of the world around us, and we can apply it to the conflicted thoughts in our consciousness. Either way, we're moving on—centered and ready for the challenges ahead.

> "Then I was given a measuring rod like a staff, and I was told, 'Come and measure the temple of God and the altar and those who worship there, but do not measure the court outside the temple; leave that out, for it is given over to the nations, and they will trample over the holy city for forty-two months.'"

—Rev. 11:1-2

This seems to be a pointless exercise with which to continue our journey. Why should we measure the temple? What will that accomplish?

To the first readers of the Revelation, in the years immediately after the armies of Rome destroyed the Temple in Jerusalem, the answer would have been obvious: to regain what we have lost. We can approach the passage metaphysically by remembering Jesus' teaching that we *are* the temple. We need to know our own spiritual center—that Presence of God within us that attracts and empowers thoughts that support our commitment. The rest of us—"the court outside the temple"—are still holy because we are fully an expression of the divine. But that part of us will be given over to the needs of being human. What's important is that we recognize, acknowledge and fully understand the temple of God that we truly are.

> "And I will grant my two witnesses authority to prophesy for one thousand two hundred and sixty days, wearing sackcloth." These are the two olive trees and the two lampstands that stand before the Lord of the earth. And if anyone wants to harm them, fire pours from their mouth and consumes their foes; anyone who wants to harm them must be killed in this manner. They have authority to shut the sky, so that no rain may fall during the days of their prophesying, and they have authority over the waters to turn them into blood, and to strike the earth with every kind of plague, as often as they desire."
>
> —Rev. 11:3-6

These two witnesses are never identified further. They are often associated with Moses and Elijah, the two figures from Hebrew history who appear with Jesus in the three Gospel accounts of the Transfiguration (Mt. 17:1-8, Mk. 9:2-8, Lk. 9:23-27). Why? Well, no apparent reason—except for convenience.

Their deeper meaning is found in the next sentence. They are "olive trees"—symbols of peace and divine promise—and lampstands—firm bases for the shining of spiritual light. Their powers seem very aggressive, but only for "anyone who wants to harm them." Representing earthly affirmations of the divine power, they properly understood that power can transform the world into a new kingdom of heaven. Misunderstood, it can and will have a destructive impact upon the false illusions we insist on embracing.

They are wearing sackcloth, symbolizing their message of "repentance," which literally means "think again" and calls us to make new choices in terms of the thoughts in mind we affirm as our beliefs. Their prophetic term is "one thousand, two hundred and sixty days," which is a number used frequently throughout the Revelation in various forms. Sometimes it is expressed as 40 months, sometimes as three and a half years. It's always the same thing—a representation of a long but finite period of time.

> "When they have finished their testimony, the beast that comes up from the bottomless pit will make war on them and conquer them and kill them, and their dead bodies will lie in the street of the great city that is prophetically called Sodom and Egypt, where also their Lord was crucified. For three and a half days members of the peoples and tribes and languages and nations will gaze at their dead bodies and refuse to let them be placed in a tomb; and the inhabitants of the earth will gloat over them and celebrate and exchange presents, because these two prophets had been a torment to the inhabitants of the earth."

—Rev. 11:7-10

So peace, spiritual promise and light will be attacked by the negative energy that emerges from the "bottomless pit" of our belief in duality and limitation. We sometimes call this destructive process "getting real." It involves believing the illusion is the only reality. It sees any kind of spiritual understanding as a useless attempt to avoid the harsh and competitive nature of life.

This will seem to be a good thing for a period of time. It will feel very freeing; our thoughts will rejoice and make merry because, frankly, all that religious stuff was becoming a major irritation. Most of us can readily identify with this process of "killing the messengers" because we felt stifled by their message as it was interpreted for us—a message of sin, obedience and punishment.

> "But after the three and a half days, the breath of life from God entered them, and they stood on their feet, and those who saw them were terrified. Then they heard a loud voice from heaven saying to them, 'Come up here!' And they went up to heaven in a cloud while their enemies watched them. At that moment there was a great earthquake, and a tenth of the city fell; seven thousand people were killed in the earthquake, and the rest were terrified and gave glory to the God of heaven."
>
> —Rev. 11:11-13

I think most of us can easily relate to this part of the vision too. We may live for a period of time without the olive trees/lampstands and the spiritual dimension they offer to the challenges we face. Even our achievements during this time feel less rich and meaningful without the higher perspective offered by these witnesses.

The time comes when these spiritual witnesses are revived—but not as religious laws concerned with human behavior. Spiritual peace, promise and illumination are now centered in heaven—in our own innate Oneness with the divine. No longer are we forced to obey rules imposed from without; we now claim our own creative power. The immediate result of that new perspective can seem devastating; a lot of thoughts based on old beliefs have to fall. There is a demanding process involved in aligning ourselves with the new. It's frightening and wonderful. We move forward.

> "The second woe has passed. The third woe is coming very soon."
>
> —Rev. 11:14

To recap: We have experienced two "woes" from the bottomless pit of our own negative thoughts. The locusts of old, deeply rooted fears were briefly painful, but they dissolved in the light of new possibility. The pseudo-logical negativity of the beast killed the witnesses of spiritual peace and understanding for a time, but since death is merely the ultimate illusion, these witnesses revived at the appropriate time and went straight to heaven—the spiritual consciousness that we now know is alive within us. So far, so good.

> "Then the seventh angel blew his trumpet, and there were loud voices in heaven, saying, 'The kingdom of the world has become the kingdom of our Lord and of his Messiah, and he will reign for ever and ever.'
>
> Then the twenty-four elders who sit on their thrones before God fell on their faces and worshiped God, singing, 'We give you thanks, Lord God Almighty, who are and who were, for you have taken your great power and begun to reign. The nations raged, but your wrath has come, and the time for judging the dead, for rewarding your servants, the prophets and saints and all who fear your name, both small and great, and for destroying those who destroy the earth.'
>
> Then God's temple in heaven was opened, and the ark of his covenant was seen within his temple; and there

were flashes of lightning, rumblings, peals of thunder, an earthquake, and heavy hail."

—Rev. 11:15-19

"The kingdom of the world has become the kingdom of our Lord and his Christ, and he shall reign for ever and ever." Could there be a more joyful statement of spiritual truth? It might be tempting to think the journey is over; we've arrived at our destination.

No. The Christ has "begun to reign" in our consciousness. This new spiritual awareness must be carefully nurtured. It is going to have a tremendous impact on the cacophony of competing thoughts in our mind, and on the manifestations of those thoughts in the world around us. Lightning, thunder, earthquakes—there are many challenges still ahead.

But we have made the most crucial step. We have remembered the witnesses to spiritual truth we thought we had destroyed, and we have discovered we both need and want the promise of their true message. Because we are newly committed to the journey, we can see in the distance our only goal—the presence of God in the temple. Our journey to that goal may be detoured and delayed by our own fears and confusion. But we can now know for certain there is no chance we will fail!

Thoughts on Step 11: Sensing Things to Come

I think what this step offers us to carry forward on our journey is the simple but essential fact that challenges are an integral part of the spiritual process to which we have committed ourselves. We have been trained and taught to see challenges as proof either that there *is* no spiritual process at work, or that we are doing it all wrong.

These two different—and equally false—beliefs represent the last bastion of the negative energy of the bottomless pit. They are the two great lies intended to discourage us from proceeding any further by using our own positive efforts against us.

The first false belief is the one used by those who profess to believe there is no God. If there were, they ask, why is the world in the state it is? How could a God allow good people to suffer and evil people to succeed? If God is love, then why are so many people in the world hungry, homeless, sick and alone? How could God allow a holocaust to happen or a tidal wave to kill tens of thousands of people?

One religious response to questions such as these is to affirm that such negative consequences are a deliberate choice by a judgmental God angry at disobedient behavior.

But to explain negative consequences as divine punishment requires silly suppositions and ridiculous twists of logic. Some fundamentalist ministers, for example, have attributed natural disasters such as hurricanes to the presence of homosexuals in nearby large cities. They attributed the more than 3,000 deaths on 9/11 to the same punishing deity, angry at liberals in the United States government.

So does that mean all those who died at the World Trade Center and the Pentagon on that tragic day were sinners who deserved their fate? Are the tens of thousands who die in a tsunami or other force of nature singled out for punishment? Or are we to believe in a God so angry that he just lashes out willy-nilly at anyone who happens to be in his way?

I really think this kind of fundamentalist absurdity does more damage to true spiritual understanding on our planet than a thousand beasts from a thousand bottomless pits could ever hope to accomplish.

We respectfully apply the name *God* to the energy that is all of life. It is an energy of infinite possibility. It contains all potential. It will express according to our faith, as Jesus taught and demonstrated time and time again. If we choose to believe in unconditional love, that is what we create. If we choose to take that same divine energy of love and express it as jealousy, possessiveness, even hatred, our free will allows us to do that; and that will become our experience.

God expresses as absolute law, according to knowable rhythms and energies. We create according to the extent to which we work *with* that law in an energy of love, or resist that law in an energy of fear.

This leads to the second false belief that may try to distract us from our spiritual focus: If everything negative isn't the will of God, then clearly it's all our fault. If we are experiencing challenges—individually or collectively—it's because we are "doing it wrong"—we are making bad choices, and we have wandered far from the path of righteousness and happiness.

This is a trickier idea to deal with because it comes cloaked in the appearance of truth. If I am experiencing challenge, and I no longer believe it to be a punishment from God inflicted specifically on me as a judgment for my behavior, then I must be creating the challenge myself. Well, yes. And no.

The difficulty here lies in the assumption that if I were "doing it right," there would be no challenges in my life. If I were perfectly aligned with divine energy, everything in my life would be perfect. My challenges and discomforts are a measure of how far out of alignment I am with my Source. I don't think that's true.

If our only spiritual purpose were to be eternally happy and challenge-free, we would never have come into human form in the first place. It's only in this illusion of duality that fear, unhappiness and conflict are experienced. We once believed that this was precisely the point—we were condemned to these human lives as a punishment for disobedience. We have grown beyond that severely limited understanding of spiritual purpose. This leaves us with the profoundly important question of why, in fact, we are here—eternal spiritual beings locked in a limited human experience.

It makes no sense to assume that we came here because we thought we'd be happier in this experience of duality and limitation than in the realm of pure spirit that is our true home. If we are one with Divine Mind—and we are—we could never be that naïve. So if we're not here as punishment, and we're not here to find happiness, then why?

We're here to create. We're here to continue the infinite activity of God called *creation*, which isn't something that happened and was complete at some specific time in the past. There is no past in spirit. Creation is happening now—and it's happening through us. And creation requires resistance. Challenges are not a sign we're doing something wrong. Challenges are the sign we are doing something right—we are resisting negative illusions and choosing spiritual truth.

This is the essence of the creative process we signed on for when we came into human form. We enter fully aware of our identity as spiritual beings. Soon, however, the surprising density of this experience of mortality causes us to forget our spiritual truth, distracted and even frightened by the mysteries of apparent duality. At some point, we begin to remember again, and it becomes a Hero's Journey of epic proportions to struggle through the fog of forgetfulness and reclaim our creative truth.

It's that struggle through the fog that gives rise to challenge and conflict. But it's also that struggle that precisely defines our spiritual purpose.

To focus on avoiding all struggle and living lives of calm acceptance is to totally miss the purpose that brought us here. That's fine—we all have times, perhaps whole lifetimes, when we need to rest from our creative efforts. But we can't stay in stasis forever—and we can't insist that these periods of calm are, in fact, the Promised Land or kingdom of heaven.

Our spiritual way forward is a process of challenge, choice and expansive growth. These beasts and locusts from the bottomless pits within us are neither punishment from God nor signs we're doing something wrong. They are the very definition of our spiritual purpose.

MEDITATION

I AM awake today to the spiritual witnesses that populate my life. Wherever my path may lead me, I see joyful and abundant support for the spiritual purpose that guides me forward.

Questions for Discussion

1. If you are to "measure your temple" by appreciating qualities from your own religious past, what is on your list? What do you appreciate from your early religious training, even if it isn't entirely compatible with your beliefs today?

2. Who or what are the "witnesses" in your own consciousness? What spiritual message do they carry?

3. How do fear-based negative thoughts try to counteract the spiritual witnesses? What is their most consistent message?

4. How are you able to remember the spiritual witnesses, even when the beast is at its loudest?

Step 12

MEETING THE ACTORS

It's time now to meet some of the major players in this feverish drama. It will be tempting—and easy—to identify them with familiar images of "good" and "evil" from earlier beliefs. But we are experiencing everything at a much deeper level now, and we can no longer settle for easy answers to challenging questions. Expressions of light and shadow can't be judged and labeled according to a belief in duality. We must face them all with the same affirmative prayer: Show me the good!

> "A great portent appeared in heaven: a woman clothed with the sun, with the moon under her feet, and on her head a crown of twelve stars. She was pregnant and was crying out in birthpangs, in the agony of giving birth."

—Rev. 12:1-2

Christians today—especially those of the Roman Catholic faith—would quickly associate this woman with the Virgin Mary, mother of Jesus. That's a valid connection, but it's not likely to be exactly what the author intended, since Mary did not yet play a significant role in the imagery and teaching of the church at that time.

We have already met the personification of God as Law in the vision's first image—the "son of man, clothed with a long robe and with a golden girdle round his breast" (Rev. 1:13), who sends forth the messages of empowerment that awaken the seven centers of spiritual energy within us. We are now encountering God as Love, the feminine aspect of the divine. She is pregnant with the Christ, the expression of our own innate divinity that is seeking to be born into the world.

Since both images of the divine are aspects of our own consciousness, it is within us that this birth—and the surrounding drama—is to occur. This divine urge to create will cause us pain, but it is expressing an energy of infinite light, greater than even the sun, moon and stars of the first creation.

> "Then another portent appeared in heaven: a great red dragon, with seven heads and ten horns, and seven diadems on his heads. His tail swept down a third of the stars of heaven and threw them to the earth."
>
> —Rev. 12:3-4

This seven-headed dragon is also contained within our own consciousness. It represents what traditional Christians call the Devil, what *A Course in Miracles* calls the ego. It's an expression of our ignorance of the Presence of God as our true reality and the fear-based choices we make as a result of having forgotten who we are. As we will see moving forward, this great dragon is the metaphysical ringmaster of the entire unfolding drama. Every expression of shadow energy, both in our own minds and in the world around us, comes from this dragon's fearful insistence on the limitations of duality.

How powerful is it? Well, as we will also see, that depends entirely on us. This fierce dragon, with seven heads of spiritual denial and crowns of earthly rule, is precisely as powerful as we believe it to be.

> "Then the dragon stood before the woman who was about to bear a child, so that he might devour her child as soon as it was born. And she gave birth to a son,

a male child, who is to rule all the nations with a rod
of iron. But her child was snatched away and taken to
God and to his throne; and the woman fled into the
wilderness, where she has a place prepared by God, so
that there she can be nourished for one thousand two
hundred sixty days."

—Rev. 12:4-6

This is the transformative event of the entire Revelation—
the painful and thrilling birth in us of Christ awareness.
Nothing is more dreaded by the dragon of fear than our awakening to the truth of our Christ identity and divine empowerment, so it stands guard, ready to devour the newborn Christ
Consciousness before we can truly experience and embrace it.

Of course, the dragon of dualistic illusion cannot destroy
the Christ of eternal truth. The newborn awareness within us is
protected by the infinite Presence and Power of God—as is the
creative energy that has just given birth. There will be consequences to be faced in consciousness as a result of the birth, and
our tentative new awareness is protected for whatever amount
of mortal time we need to face them.

"And war broke out in heaven; Michael and his angels
fought against the dragon. The dragon and his angels
fought back, but they were defeated, and there was no
longer any place for them in heaven. The great dragon
was thrown down, that ancient serpent, who is called
the Devil and Satan, the deceiver of the whole world—
he was thrown down to the earth, and his angels were
thrown down with him."

—Rev. 12:7-9

This is the only reference in the Bible to the familiar story
of a war in heaven and the banishment of Satan and his min-
ions. The "bad angels" are "thrown down to the earth." In other

versions—especially the vivid narrative of *Paradise Lost* by the blind English poet John Milton—it is to the lower depths of hell that the dragon and his angels are condemned.

Metaphysically, we might expect that the birth of a new dimension of Christ awareness within us would inevitably lead to a life of peace and contentment. That expectation is what makes this chapter so important in terms of our own spiritual process. The truth is that, just as Jesus' own baptismal step into Christ Consciousness was followed at once by the temptations in the wilderness, so will our own spiritual birth awaken and arouse the fear-based energies that have been comfortably calling the shots through much of our lives. By anticipating this reaction, we can avoid the danger of being thrown off course by the intense energy it represents.

"Then I heard a loud voice in heaven, proclaiming, 'Now have come the salvation and the power and the kingdom of our God and the authority of his Messiah, for the accuser of our comrades has been thrown down, who accuses them day and night before our God. But they have conquered him by the blood of the Lamb and by the word of their testimony, for they did not cling to life even in the face of death. Rejoice then, you heavens and those who dwell in them! But woe to the earth and the sea, for the devil has come down to you with great wrath, because he knows that his time is short!'"

—Rev. 12:10-12

Historically, this passage is clearly aimed at those early followers of Jesus who were being arrested, tortured and subjected to painful death by Roman authorities because of their faith. It was understandably important in the early church that these martyrs have a place of honor in the kingdom to come. They are seen as soldiers in the great cosmic battle, and the promise is that, although they have died, they are truly the victors over the forces of Satan.

The same promise is equally important for us through the spiritual process that engages us. The "blood of the Lamb" and the "word" are the newly-realized energy and understanding represented by the birth of Christ awareness. This spiritual energy has already won the battle, although the fear-based energies in our mortal minds are still loud, shrill and chaotic in their efforts to dissuade us from our new commitment. The devil "knows that his time is short," and we are called to know this same truth as we move through the challenges that lie ahead.

> "So when the dragon saw that he had been thrown down to the earth, he pursued the woman who had given birth to the male child. But the woman was given the two wings of the great eagle, so that she could fly from the serpent into the wilderness, to her place where she is nourished for a time, and times, and half a time."
>
> —Rev. 12:13-14

The battle already decided in heaven—in spiritual consciousness—is still being acted out in our mortal experience. But we are now awake and aware, consciously linked with the creative spiritual Power that is our assurance of victory. Both the child of Christ awareness and the creative energy from which it emerged are absolutely safe for the period of time required for us to deal with the challenges of dualistic conflict.

> "Then from his mouth the serpent poured water like a river after the woman, to sweep her away with the flood. But the earth came to the help of the woman; it opened its mouth and swallowed the river that the dragon had poured from his mouth. Then the dragon

> was angry with the woman, and went off to make war
> on the rest of her children, those who keep the com-
> mandments of God and hold the testimony of Jesus."
>
> —Rev. 12:15-17

The negative energy of fear and angry judgment flow from the dragon "like a river," seeking to sweep away the creative energy that is birthing our expanded understanding. And help comes from a surprising place—from the earth itself, home of the dualistic life experience that so often seems to be working with the dragon. The implication is important, I think. We are not to think of an inherent conflict between our spiritual truth and this dualistic earthly illusion. Remember our foundation belief—One Presence, One Power. The energy of God is every-where, and it is always an energy eager to support our spiritual endeavors. With "Show me the Good" as our only mantra, we can find blessings and deep understanding in all aspects of this human experience.

Thoughts on Step 12: Meeting the Actors

There are three important questions that must be addressed in any system of spiritual belief: What is the nature of the power we call *God*? What is the true nature of humanity? What is the relationship between God and humanity?

The first half of the Revelation to John—the first 11 of its 22 chapters—have addressed the first two questions. God is, simply, all that is. God is the energy of all life—an energy of omniscience, omnipresence, omnipotence. God is an energy of infinite love. The true nature of humankind is that we are spir-itual beings, one with our divine Source, engaged in a human illusion of separation and duality.

Chapter 12 opens the door to considering the third question, and it is here that so many interpretations of the Revelation go seriously off track. In order to fully understand its message, we must approach it with open hearts and open minds. If we come to it with preconceptions based on what we've been taught or have already chosen to believe, we can find support for those already-entrenched ideas. But we will miss the radical new sense of understanding and empowerment the Revelation—and, indeed the very teachings of Jesus Christ—offer in terms of our relationship to the divine.

Many traditionalists explain the relationship between God and humanity in terms of not one, but two, falls from grace. They believe, on two separate occasions, creatures created by God rebelled against the divine order, according to which God expresses in the kingdom of heaven. These rebellions so angered God that the creatures were cast out of heaven as punishment.

The first of these dramatic rebellions involved Satan and those angels he was able to muster to his side in his determination to overthrow God in heaven. As noted above, this is not really a biblical story, although many who revere the Bible are sure that it's described in great detail, somewhere in its pages.

It's not. It's a story that the Jews exiled to Babylon apparently learned from the followers of Zoroaster, among whom they lived there. Intrinsic to Zoroastrianism is a belief in the spiritual truth of duality and in life as a constant war between the forces of good and the forces of evil. When those Jews were permitted to return from exile, they brought with them the seeds of a belief in spiritual duality, which became nonbiblical stories and legends about a great war in heaven. It's only in the Revelation to John that these stories find their way into scripture.

The second story of a great fall is, indeed, found in the Bible—specifically in the Book of Genesis. It is the familiar story of Adam, Eve, the serpent and the fruit of the Tree of Knowledge of Good and Evil. As with all the early stories of Genesis (up to the introduction of Abram and the beginning of a recorded history), it was never intended as a literal record of facts but as an explanation of spiritual truth in terms clear to the simplest of human minds.

The basics of the plot as traditionally understood are familiar to us all. Adam and Eve are given carte blanche in the Garden of Eden, except for the Tree of the Knowledge of Good and Evil, of which they are told not to eat. The serpent—traditionally understood to be Satan in disguise—tempts Eve with promises of knowledge, power and eternal life. She eats and persuades Adam to eat as well. As punishment, they are banished from the Garden, into lives of pain and lack. The traditional answer to the third question, then, is that the relationship between God and humankind is one of disobedience, anger, punishment and enforced separation.

If we come to the Revelation with a firm faith in these stories, we can certainly find ways to validate them in its unfolding drama. People even find such validation in the teachings of Jesus, which is really a stretch given the loving, intimate, empowering relationship he describes between Creator and created.

If we are willing to set aside what we think we already know about our relationship with the divine, and let the Revelation speak for itself, an entirely different story begins to emerge. There is no denying the often painful experiences of conflict and ignorance intrinsic to our humanity. But there is no sense of punishment involved; there is rather the innate awareness that these experiences are precisely our spiritual work to do. And there is no sense of separation from God as a fact of our mortality. How can we possibly be separate from a God of omnipresence? How can even the forces of Satan occupy a realm called *hell*, which—in the old Baltimore catechism, at least—is defined as the "absence of God"?

Traditional religious belief—as separate from spiritual understanding—really seems to affirm the reality of this human experience of duality. We are, indeed, separate from God. God is angry, and we are being punished. Our only hope is to work ourselves back into good favor with God so that, when we leave this mortal realm at death, we will be allowed back into the kingdom/garden.

It is this underlying belief that we have "fallen" from an exalted spiritual place, and that this human experience is intended as a form of punishment, that allows a hierarchical religious structure to govern our lives, passing down to us from on high instructions about what God demands of us. Small wonder that the Roman emperor Constantine found the three-centuries-old Christian Church so easy to embrace. Its underlying structure and top-down control was identical to that of the Empire itself!

The true—and truly empowering—answer to the third question is that the relationship between Creator and created is one of complete and intimate Oneness. Our purpose in this human adventure is not blind obedience, but loving creation. We are here to extend the experience of God as far as we possibly can.

As we will see in chapters to come, that purpose will generate resistance and confusion in consciousness and, because we are creative beings, that resistance and confusion will express in the world around us. We are not to accept that, nor are we to avoid it. We are to transform it.

MEDITATION

Today I AM open and eager to receive the blessings of the world as my spiritual path continues to unfold. Instead of challenges and resistance, I see opportunities to express my creative power and transform the world. I AM one with the infinite love of the divine, and I see that love reflected in everyone and everything I meet.

Questions for Discussion

1. Discuss and/or journal about the image of the pregnant woman. She is given no real personality in the Revelation. Is she simply a blank slate? If not, what thoughts or feelings might she be holding?

2. What is the meaning to you of the "rod of iron" with which the male child is to rule? Does it suggest cruelty? Or something else? Is it significant that this firstborn Christ energy is male? Why, or why not?

3. Note that after the great war, Satan in this version of the story is not cast into hell, but "thrown down to the earth." Is this a significant difference? Why?

4. In what ways can "the earth" be of help on our spiritual path?

5. How do you answer the three questions? To what extent are you free from old belief in a fall? Are there ways in which those old beliefs are still at work?

Step 13

RECOGNIZING TWO BEASTS

S o the battle that was first waged in heaven—in consciousness—is now being fought in the tangible world. This
allows the Revelation to speak to its first readers about
the challenges and conflicts of the day—coded, of course, so
only those who understood the symbolism would understand
the full message. It's because of the necessity of communicat-
ing in code that Chapter 13 has become so misunderstood and
feared through the years.

> "And I saw a beast rising out of the sea, having ten
> horns and seven heads; and on its horns were ten dia-
> dems, and on its heads were blasphemous names. And
> the beast that I saw was like a leopard, its feet were like
> a bear's, and its mouth was like a lion's mouth. And
> the dragon gave it his power and his throne and great
> authority. One of its heads seemed to have received a
> death-blow, but its mortal wound had been healed."

—Rev. 13:1-3

The imagery in Chapter 13 draws heavily from the proph-
ecies recorded in the Book of Daniel (particularly Chapter 7).
The earlier prophet describes four beasts, and at that time, 600
years prior to the Revelation, they were meant to represent the
empires of Babylonia, Persia, the Medes and the Greeks—all of
which were competing for temporal power. In the Revelation to
John, the four beasts are combined into one beast with qualities

of all four. This megabeast from the sea is the Roman Empire, which has, indeed, absorbed the lands and peoples of all four earlier kingdoms. The crowned heads are the various emperors with "blasphemous names" because they insisted on being worshiped as gods.

Today I think we can see the beast from the sea as representing the false belief system under which we live in this illusion of duality, until the birth of Christ Consciousness allows us to see the beast as false. Interestingly, this beast has no power of its own; it receives all the power it has from the dragon—the negative, fear-based energy that insists on our separation from God.

> "In amazement the whole earth followed the beast. They worshiped the dragon, for he had given his authority to the beast, and they worshiped the beast, saying, 'Who is like the beast, and who can fight against it?'"
>
> —Rev. 13:3-4

Certainly the entire known world at the time of the Revelation lived in thrall to the Roman Empire. Like it or hate it, the Empire was simply a reality to be accepted. "You can't fight City Hall." In accepting the beast, however, the people were in effect "worshiping the dragon" by believing without question in the message of separation and powerlessness that allowed the beast to rule.

Today we can see this beast, not just as whatever government we may have over us, but as the entire, elaborate system of rules and regulations that encourage us to put our faith in this human experience instead of in our spiritual truth. This beast has expanded its reach throughout the years, if not its power. All the scientific discoveries and measurements of past centuries have become a part of the mindset that "knows what it knows" and believes only what is tangible and provable in the domain of senses and intellect in which our belief is centered.

> "The beast was given a mouth uttering haughty and blasphemous words, and it was allowed to exercise authority for forty-two months. It opened its mouth to utter blasphemies against God, blaspheming his name and his dwelling, that is, those who dwell in heaven. Also it was allowed to make war on the saints and to conquer them. It was given authority over every tribe and people and language and nation, and all the inhabitants of the earth will worship it, everyone whose name has not been written from the foundation of the world in the book of life of the Lamb that was slaughtered."

—Rev. 13:5-8

Again, we understand the qualities attributed here to the symbolic Roman Empire to describe with great accuracy our struggle today with the dictates of the world. For a measurable period of time—the symbolic 42 months again—the beast will pretty much run things. It's underlying purpose is to keep us locked in a sense of powerlessness, helpless victims of "the way things are." To that end, it will attack any spiritual belief that threatens its control, in every "tribe and people and language and nation."

The "book of life" has already been mentioned as the living, eternal record of those souls who are awake to their true spiritual identity. Because they know themselves to be eternal beings, even the illusion of death cannot touch or frighten them.

> "Let anyone who has an ear listen: If you are to be taken captive, into captivity you go; if you kill

with the sword, with the sword you must be killed.
Here is a call for the endurance and faith of the saints."

—Rev. 13:9-10

In this helpful aside, the Revelation offers us a bit of practical advice on applying spiritual principle to the challenges of this beast. It involves simply knowing who we truly are and how the creative power of God expresses through us. The essential truth is we will experience according to our beliefs. If we are taken captive, it will be because we have chosen to believe in the possibility of captivity. As Job exclaims, "That which I greatly fear has come upon me!" (Job 3:25). Fear is an especially insidious form of creative empowerment; by choosing to fear something or someone, we are granting it a power over us—and that power we fear will manifest in our lives.

And then comes another reminder of "How It Works" when it comes to making right choices. "If you kill with the sword, with the sword you must be killed." This is not new information, of course. Note this powerful response when the prophet Jeremiah asks the Lord where his people are to go: "Thus says the Lord: Those who are for pestilence, to pestilence, and those who are for the sword, to the sword; those who are for famine, to famine, and those who are for captivity, to captivity" (Jer. 15:2). And at the time of Jesus' arrest, when a follower draws his sword to defend him by attacking a servant of the High Priest, Jesus lovingly issues the same warning: "Put your sword back in its place, for all who take the sword will perish by the sword" (Mt. 26:52).

The message is clear. By choosing to do battle with our perceived enemies, we are giving them a measure of our own power. It's by rising above the conflict, above the dimension of anger or fear, that we know ourselves to be an infinite power that cannot be threatened or attacked.

"Then I saw another beast that rose out of the earth; it had two horns like a lamb and it spoke like a dragon. It exercises all the authority of the first beast on its behalf, and it makes the earth and its inhabitants worship the first beast, whose mortal wound had been healed. It performs great signs, even making fire come down from heaven to earth in the sight of all; and by the signs that it is allowed to perform on behalf of the beast, it deceives the inhabitants of earth, telling them to make an image for the beast that had been wounded by the sword and yet lived; and it was allowed to give breath to the image of the beast so that the image of the beast could even speak and cause those who would not worship the image of the beast to be killed."

—Rev. 13:11-15

Oh, geez! Another beast already! Can't we dispense with the beast from the sea first before we turn to the beast from the land? Well, it seems logical; but logic rarely has much to do with spiritual progress. The two beasts are so interconnected—both with each other and with the dragon that empowers them both—that we need to deal with them both.

If the beast from the sea represents the illusions of duality presented as real, then what is left for the beast from the land? Well, there's no kind and gentle way to say this. The beast from the land—aka the false prophet—represents those *religious* beliefs that try to control us with teachings of sin, punishment and general unworthiness. The first beast claims total knowledge of how our human lives are meant to express. This second beast extends that false self-assurance to our relationship with God. This is the beast that loves to repeat the stories of the two falls from grace we discussed earlier. It presents itself as the Lamb (of God) but speaks with the voice of the dragon.

What's interesting here, I think, is the clear indication that, while this second beast pretends to have a direct connection to God, it is in fact in constant support of the first beast. It "deceives those who dwell on earth" with impressive, pseudo-religious signs and wonders. And yet its true purpose is to reinforce the sense of weakness and separation that is the essence of the first beast's interpretation of our human condition.

> "Also it causes all, both small and great, both rich and poor, both free and slave, to be marked on the right hand or the forehead, so that no one can buy or sell who does not have the mark, that is, the name of the beast or the number of its name. This calls for wisdom: let anyone with understanding calculate the number of the beast, for it is the number of a person. Its number is six hundred sixty-six."
>
> —Rev. 13:16-18

"This calls for wisdom" indeed—and wisdom has been in short supply when it comes to understanding this brief passage. Throughout the 20 centuries between us and the Revelation, the number 666 has been treated with superstitious fear. Buildings can't use it as a street number, for example, because people refuse to live at that address. It's "the number of the beast," which is interpreted as meaning it's the sign of Satan.

All of this anxiety about a passage that immediately follows a forceful reminder that it's our own fear-based faith in negative energy that gives it power in our lives! It's no wonder there are stories about powerful negative consequences associated with 666. It's our belief that negative consequences will happen that brings them into being.

The Christian-believing Jews to whom the Revelation was first directed were highly skilled at numerology—finding meaning, patterns and hidden codes in the use of certain numerals. The many books of Scripture, from beginning to end, are rife with numerological significance. The numbers seven, 12 and 40, in particular were understood to have great spiritual significance.

These early readers would have immediately understood that 666 is a numerical expression equivalent to "Nero Caesar." We have already mentioned the superstitious belief, common at the time, that the hated Nero had not really died. Like Elvis, he was rumored to have faked his death to escape the consequences of his insane choices. It was believed that he was somewhere to the east of the Empire, amassing a large army that would one day conquer the forces of Rome and restore the age of barbarism for which Nero was known. It's the fear that Nero had secret followers, known only to each other, working to prepare the way for his army's imminent arrival that generates the coded warning that ends Chapter 13.

Thoughts on Step 13: Recognizing Two Beasts

It's unfortunate that Chapter 13 has become notorious for all the wrong reasons. The two beasts, the great dragon, the secret signs and signals, the "number of the beast"—it's amazing that Hollywood hasn't converted the drama into an effects-laden 3-D spectacular. It's all vivid and entertaining—but it's not the affirmation of duality and conflict so many insist on finding. In fact, it's just the opposite.

Except for a few helpful interjections from a different perspective, this entire chapter is concerned with the illusion of duality and separation that the dragon of fear and ignorance manufactures in an attempt to maintain its powerful hold on our unawakened minds. The Presence of God, the newly born Christ Consciousness—these are nowhere to be found. Spiritual truth does not engage in a fight to the finish with the dark shadow forces of fear. Why should the truth treat lies as equals, worthy of being challenged?

We've already been told in spiritual consciousness that the dragon can only hold sway for a brief period of time. Now that we are awake to our true Christ nature, we can no longer believe in the lies of the two beasts—both empowered by the dragon of negativity. Why, then, describe them at all? Why not just ignore them, and wait for their dramas to play themselves out?

The answer, I think, lies in the fact that we are not engaged in this process—this Hero's Journey—just for ourselves alone. We may now be relatively immune to the combined powers of the two beasts, but many others are still in their sway. The more aware and observant we are able to be, the more we may be able to recognize the negative energy flow and help to lovingly dissolve it. None of us will be unadulterated expressions of pure spirit as long as we continue to express our spirit selves within the apparent limitations of a human experience. But we can accomplish a great deal by staying conscious, and by fearlessly sharing our love and awareness at every opportunity.

This is the essence of prayer. Effective prayer requires that we recognize the effects of the two beasts expressing as negative energy—in our own lives or in the lives of others. We don't fight that energy; we don't even judge it. We simply affirm the truth, and align our faith *with* that truth, and allow the energy of the divine to dissolve the effects of the illusion.

This is also the essence of the Warrior archetype that represents our next role as the Hero's Journey continues to unfold. It's not that we are to take up swords and go to war against the perceived power of the beasts. "Resist not evil," Jesus taught (Mt. 5:39), and as always he meant what he said. The simple exercise of faith required to believe that there is something of the beasts that needs to be resisted strengthens the beasts' power. It also creates a stronger beast experience for ourselves and those for whom we pray. There is a world of difference between praying that an illness goes away and praying that one's innate perfect health be made manifest. The first increases the reality of the illness by believing it exists and needs to be resisted. The second sees past the illusion of illness without giving the illusion of the empowerment of our fearful faith. It instead brings forward into expression the spiritual truth that does not need to fight against illusions.

And so we are to continue observing the effects of the beasts in the world around us—not fearfully, and not judgmentally, but with an affirmative awareness that nothing in the illusion can threaten our innate spiritual power. We don't deny the effects of the beasts of human ignorance and the misuse of power. We see clearly the damage they cause in our own lives and in the world we share. We embrace every opportunity to replace the ignorance with spiritual truth; the misuse of power with unconditional love. We firmly resist every urging to allow the beasts any more power than they already have been given. We decrease that power at every opportunity.

We are no longer victims, nor are we warriors of fear-based resistance and angry attack. We are the Warrior, secure in the power of God, standing firm in our innate Oneness with each other and with the divine. We appreciate the beasts for the opportunities they offer to replace ignorance with truth and fear with love. We are not discouraged by appearances; we are centered in faith.

MEDITATION

Today I choose to calmly and quietly observe the drama of the two beasts unfolding in the world around me. I AM secure in knowing there is nothing to fear. I AM grateful to be guided to opportunities to replace the illusions of the beasts with the infinite light of the Christ. I AM a peaceful, centered spiritual Warrior, and it is a perfect day.

Questions for Discussion

1. What beliefs or areas of "knowing" have become false gods that we tend to worship, after the manner of the first beast? What is the good to be gained by expanding our knowledge of this human experience? What is the spiritual challenge?

2. We're told of the first beast that "it was allowed to exercise authority." Who allows it? Why?

3. What do you know in your own life of a beast that looks like a lamb and speaks like a dragon? The second beast's primary purpose seems to be to increase the power of the first beast by impressing people with signs and magic. Since both beasts are powered from the dragon, what is the dragon trying to accomplish by working through both at once?

4. Why does the beast control the process of buying and selling, as well as the distinction between slavery and freedom? What does that suggest about the economic system in general?

Step 14

REAFFIRMING THE GOOD

Are we having fun yet? We should be because we are making great progress on our Hero's Journey. And now the vision grants us another interlude in which we can rest, reaffirm the truth that anchors us, and embrace the absolute guarantee that a joyful marriage of our human and spiritual natures lies just ahead.

> "Then I looked, and there was the Lamb, standing on Mount Zion! And with him were one hundred for-ty-four thousand who had his name and his Father's name written on their foreheads."
>
> —Rev. 14:1

For several chapters now, we have been focused exclusively on the conflict unfolding in the mortal realm. This is necessary and important. But it's even more important that we take time to realize there is another dimension within us that remains above the fray, unaffected by the drama. We have met these 144,000 before; they are the "great multitude that no one could count" (Rev. 7:9) who metaphysically represent thoughts in our consciousness. They remain with the Lamb, standing on Mount Zion, which represents Jerusalem, which in turn represents the spiritual realm within us. These thoughts and their loving power are always with us, but we have to remember to look.

> "And I heard a voice from heaven like the sound of many waters and like the sound of loud thunder; the

voice I heard was like the sound of harpists playing on their harps, and they sing a new song before the throne and before the four living creatures and before the elders. No one could learn that song except the one hundred forty-four thousand who have been redeemed from the earth. It is these who have not defiled themselves with women, for they are virgins; these follow the Lamb wherever he goes. They have been redeemed from humankind as first fruits for God and the Lamb, and in their mouth no lie was found; they are blameless."

—Rev. 14:2-5

Because Christ Consciousness has been born within us, these spiritual thoughts are able to express as a "new song" of love and creative possibility. These thoughts are described as "virgins" because they do not enter into our illusions of duality. They are "redeemed from the earth" so they live in our minds as constant affirmations of our true spiritual identity. They "follow the Lamb wherever he goes" (in a kind of spiritual reversal of Mary and her little lamb) to add their loving power to our creative process.

"Then I saw another angel flying in mid-heaven, with an eternal gospel to proclaim to those who live on the earth—to every nation and tribe and language and people. He said in a loud voice, 'Fear God and give him glory, for the hour of his judgment has come; and worship him who made heaven and earth, the sea and the springs of water.'"

—Rev. 14:6-7

These spiritual thoughts in our own consciousness are guided and empowered by angels representing ideas eternally generated from the Divine Mind of God. This first angel simply calls us to spiritual focus; we must remember always that, however dark the illusions of beasts and dragons, the Good that is God is always everywhere present. Appreciating every expression of that Good is the essential first step toward expanding it through our creative focus.

I think there are two important points to be made about this passage. First, this is "an eternal gospel" given "to every nation and tribe and language and people." There is no suggestion that only those who believe in Jesus, or who are members of a specific faith or church, are a part of this spiritual process. Second, we don't "fear God" as we would fear a rampaging beast. The word translated as "fear" rather evokes the kind of awe we feel in an old-growth forest, or a beautiful cathedral. It's an awareness that we are in the Presence of an energy far greater than ourselves.

> "Then another angel, a second, followed, saying, 'Fallen, fallen is Babylon the great! She has made all nations drink of the wine of the wrath of her fornication.'"
>
> —Rev. 14:8

If we were to return our attention to our earthly drama at this point, we would not see that "Babylon" is fallen. The two beasts, fueled by the fear-based passion of the dragon, were still holding sway when last we checked. The nations were still drinking the "wine of wrath" that is being birthed by their negative energy. This second angel of divine guidance assures us that in the kingdom of heaven, the conflict does not exist. Any energy opposed to Divine Mind is illusive at best, and its effects will not stand. As an early teacher once assured me, God is not worried about the outcome.

> "Then another angel, a third, followed them, crying with a loud voice, 'Those who worship the beast and its

image, and receive a mark on their foreheads or on their
hands, they will also drink the wine of God's wrath,
poured unmixed into the cup of his anger, and they will
be tormented with fire and sulfur in the presence of the
holy angels and in the presence of the Lamb. And the
smoke of their torment goes up forever and ever.'"

—Rev. 14:9-11

We'll discuss this whole idea of "God's wrath" in our
thoughts at the end of this chapter. A "mark on their foreheads
or on their hands" suggests two different ideas, equally important. Some people "mark" their foreheads or hands—or other
body parts—with tattoos, as a decorative way of affirming their
association with an idea or group. Those thoughts in our consciousness that choose to believe the beasts will, indeed, experience the inevitable pain caused by a refusal to learn, grow and
change.

But such marks were used in the Roman Empire to identify
slaves, which suggests there may be thoughts in consciousness
that serve the beasts out of fear—out of a belief that they have
no choice. They, too, will experience the negative consequences
of that allegiance—until they become willing to heed the guidance of the 144,000 and realize the beasts have no real power.

"There is no rest day or night for those who worship
the beast and its image and for anyone who receives
the mark of its name.

Here is a call for the endurance of the saints, those who
keep the commandments of God and hold fast to the
faith of Jesus."

—Rev. 14:11-12

Here we have a profound spiritual truth disguised as
utter simplicity. We may think it's very difficult to "keep the

commandments of God and hold fast to the faith of Jesus"—and it is, as Jesus himself recognizes frequently in the course of his ministry. To look past the illusions to the Lamb on the mountaintop, to heed the new song of our pure spiritual mind, to remove the power of our faith from the dramas of our daily lives—it ain't easy! Or so it seems from our limited human perspective.

But the work involved in expressing our Christ energy is nothing—nothing!—compared to the work involved in denying it. To insist on maintaining a negative, fear-based mindset is incredibly, painfully difficult. After all, God is everywhere present as infinite Good; so refusing to see or acknowledge this Presence requires constant vigilance. This fearful vigilance is the source of the tension and utter exhaustion that seem to be epidemic in the world today.

> "And I heard a voice from heaven saying, 'Write this: Blessed are the dead who from now on die in the Lord.' 'Yes,' says the Spirit, 'they will rest from their labors, for their deeds follow them.'"
>
> —Rev. 14:13

What does it mean to "die in the Lord?" It seems to be a contradiction in terms, since "in the Lord" we know ourselves to be eternal spiritual beings. So "to die in the Lord" is not to die at all—to see the transition we call "death" as simply another fear-based illusion. To die in Christ Consciousness is to move without fear or resistance from one dimension of spiritual expression to another. Our "deeds" will follow us because we now recognize and embrace the continuity of life that makes that possible.

> "Then I looked, and there was a white cloud, and seated on the cloud was one like the Son of Man, with a golden crown on his head, and a sharp sickle in his

hand! Another angel came out of the temple, calling with a loud voice to the one who sat on the cloud, 'Use your sickle and reap, for the hour to reap has come, because the harvest of the earth is fully ripe.' So the one who sat on the cloud swung his sickle over the earth, and the earth was reaped."

—Rev. 14:14-16

If we understand "Son of God" to describe our true identity as eternal spiritual beings, then "Son of Man" must describe that spiritual identity expressing *through* the illusions of human limitation. So it is not Jesus who is doing the reaping here—it's us!

Let's turn for a moment to the words of Jesus in the fourth chapter of the Gospel of John: "Do you not say, 'Four months more, then comes the harvest'? But I tell you, look around you, and see how the fields are ripe for harvesting. The reaper is already receiving wages and is gathering fruit for eternal life, so that sower and reaper may rejoice together. For here the saying holds true, 'one sows and another reaps.' I sent you to reap that for which you did not labor. Others have labored, and you have entered into their labor" (Jn. 4:35-38).

Could anything be clearer as a description of the creative process to which we are called? We are to look beyond appearances, to see the spiritual harvest eternally at hand, and to gather it in. I think Jesus himself is one of the "others" who labored to sow the seeds of possibility. This reaping is not a punishment, nor is it the end of the world. There will always be more to harvest. Our job is to recognize the abundant crop of infinite Good growing from the seeds of divine ideas, to claim it and clear it so more Good can grow.

"Then another angel came out of the temple in heaven, and he too had a sharp sickle. Then another angel came out from the altar, the angel who has authority over fire, and he called with a loud voice to him who had the sharp sickle, 'Use your sharp sickle and gather the clusters of the vine of the earth, for its grapes are ripe.' So the angel swung his sickle over the earth and gathered the vintage of the earth, and he threw it into the great wine press of the wrath of God. And the wine press was trodden outside the city, and blood flowed from the wine press, as high as a horse's bridle, for a distance of about two hundred miles."

—Rev. 14:17-20

There are moments in the Revelation when I suspect the John to whom it was revealed didn't entirely understand it himself. That's not surprising. Anytime we receive a divine idea from the timeless realm of spirit, we have to interpret it within the confines of a limited mindset defined by the world in which we live. As that mindset expands, however, we must allow our understanding of those ideas to expand as well. This is what makes the Bible such a powerful resource for our journey, always expressing with new insight as our awareness expands.

It seems to be only John's preconceptions that make the wine press an expression of "the wrath of God." A wine press is not a punishment for the grapes; it is an essential part of the process of transforming those grapes into wine. Wine is, indeed, a symbol of spiritual blood—the very essence of eternal life. For Roman Catholics, in particular, this analogy is very real; the wine consecrated at the Mass becomes the blood of Christ, and to receive it is to receive the life essence of the divine. It is nowhere recorded that the transubstantiated communion wine is understood as an expression of God's wrath. Rather, the image continues of reaping a ripe spiritual harvest and putting it to use as the essence of eternal life.

Thoughts on Step 14: Reaffirming the Good

If we're going to make it through the next few chapters with our faith intact, we need to understand the idea of "the wrath of God." There's no denying John sees it everywhere in the Revelation, and countless millions of people since have eagerly embraced it as the basic energy of judgment and punishment they believe the book—and, indeed, the Bible as a whole—to be describing.

In a belief system centered in duality—seeing life as a constant battle between the forces of good and the forces of evil—the idea of a wrathful God makes some degree of sense. We assume God to be wrathful against the forces intentionally aligned against him, angry about the devious ways they are leading his people astray and encouraging them to be disobedient to his law. *We* would feel wrathful if we were God and, since we tend to think of God as an infinite version of ourselves, we assume God feels the same way—only more so.

Once we affirm our first basic principle—One Presence, One Power—however, there is no longer anything for God to be wrathful against. It's all God! Whatever we are experiencing, or whatever we observe others to be experiencing, it's all a part of the Allness of God.

We don't deny the existence of painful experiences—we could scarcely maintain a belief system that ignores such a large and significant part of the human condition. We understand that, at early levels of religious awareness, we may see the pain as an expression of divine anger. But we become willing to follow the teachings of Jesus Christ to a deeper, more loving understanding of what's really going on.

The bottom line is that choices have consequences. If we consistently make negative, fear-based choices, we will experience negative, fear-based consequences as painful and scary as anything described in the Revelation. These consequences are, indeed, from God—everything is. However, they are not intended as wrathful punishment. They are intended as life lessons, to help us learn how divine law expresses in this mortal realm, so we can make more loving, creative choices—and experience more loving, creative consequences—the next time.

God is not an angry, condemning voice of pain and punishment with which we have all become familiar; that is totally the voice of the beasts. God is the "still small voice" (1 Kings 19:12) that never ceases believing in us, loving us, encouraging us to make new choices.

MEDITATION

Today I AM a harvester of spiritual good in all aspects of my human experience. My spiritual scythe is the power of appreciation. I take time to speak words of thanks and kindness, to listen with love and concern, and to know at the day's end that I have reaped a rich crop of spiritual blessings—for myself and for all others.

Questions for Discussion

1. How do you personally hear the "new song" of the 144,000 within you? What is the song saying?

2. Can you think of places or moments when you felt the sense of awe described here as "fear of God"? What quality of the divine spoke to you most strongly?

3. What does it mean to you to "die in the Lord"? How might it relate to Jesus' teaching that we must be born again?

4. In what ways have you reaped a spiritual crop that was sown by others? In addition to reaping, how might we be called to sow the seeds of future harvests?

Step 15

SINGING THE SONG OF THE LAMB

W e now have two chapters concerned with another set of spiritual sevens—seven angels with seven bowls of wrath. We're in the home stretch and we have the assurance of the visions of the previous chapter that all will indeed end well. The negative energies of judgment and fear aren't done yet. We still need to maintain the Warrior archetype against the contents of seven bowls of painful shadows from the past.

> "Then I saw another portent in heaven, great and amazing: seven angels with seven plagues, which are the last, for with them the wrath of God is ended."
>
> —Rev. 15:1

I think it's significant here that our focus is still on the dominion of heaven. We are no longer so deeply enmeshed in the seductive dramas playing out on Earth. We're still affected by them, but whatever power they still hold over us is overbalanced by the new Christ awareness that lifts us to a higher perspective.

> "And I saw what appeared to be a sea of glass mixed with fire, and those who had conquered the beast and its image and the number of its name, standing beside the sea of glass with harps of God in their hands."
>
> —Rev. 15:2

Can you imagine this scene in your mind? "Those who had conquered the beast and its image and the number of its name" are the symbolic 144,000, standing and singing beside a "sea of glass mixed with fire." It's an image both beautiful and unsettling.

This fire is clearly not to be associated with pain and punishment; it represents a process of purification that transforms everything into an expression of the kingdom. A sea of glass is an image from the prophet Ezekiel (Ezek. 1:22); it suggests that the very elements—the building blocks of creation—are transformed into a shining new dimension of eternal spirit.

> "And they sing the song of Moses, the servant of God, and the song of the Lamb: 'Great and amazing are your deeds, Lord God the Almighty! Just and true are your ways, King of the nations! Lord, who will not fear and glorify your name? For you alone are holy. All nations will come and worship before you, for your judgments have been revealed.'"
>
> —Rev. 15:3-4

This song is a combination of two hymns recorded in Hebrew scripture (Ex. 15:1-18 and Deut. 32) and attributed to the Israelites in the wilderness. They are en route to their own Promised Land—the place in consciousness where they can take ownership of their life experiences and sow the seeds of new possibility. So, too, these expressions of Christ Consciousness standing by the sea of glass are entering a new land—the kingdom of heaven—which they are creating, choice by choice, as they join together in praise of their spiritual Source.

> "After this I looked, and the temple of the tent of witness in heaven was opened, and out of the temple came

the seven angels with the seven plagues, robed in pure bright linen, with golden sashes across their chests."

—Rev. 15:5-6

The "tent of witness" was the symbolic home of the Ark of the Covenant as the Israelites moved through the wilderness. Long before the Temple was constructed in Jerusalem, the tent of witness represented the Presence of the divine in the midst of human challenges. Jesus taught that we ourselves are the temple—we are the Presence of the divine. And it's time to open the tent, to release our creative Christ nature. It should not be surprising by this stage of the journey that the result is not an immediate happy ending, but rather the release of pent-up negative energies that must be experienced and released to clear the way for the kingdom.

"Then one of the four living creatures gave the seven angels seven golden bowls full of the wrath of God, who lives forever and ever; and the temple was filled with smoke from the glory of God and from his power, and no one could enter the temple until the seven plagues of the seven angels were ended."

—Rev. 15:7-8

We first met "the four living creatures" in Chapter 4; here they continue their work of expediting the creative process. The seven angels are, as always, divine ideas emanating from Divine Mind. The golden bowls contain the final seven stages of standing fast we need to accomplish as our Hero's Journey enters its final stages.

Thoughts on Step 15: Singing the Song of the Lamb

Something very interesting begins to take shape as the Revelation to John enters its final phase. We begin to experience echoes of the earliest stages of our journey. The hymns and many of the images in this brief chapter remind us of the archetype of the Wanderer, which we left behind some time ago. We may well wonder if we've somehow taken a wrong turn.

We haven't, of course. The truth, I think, is far more interesting. It seems as we get close to the completion of one Hero's Journey, we are already feeling the stirrings of another one!

This doesn't make sense if we allow our mortal minds to imagine our spiritual journey in two-dimensional, longitudinal terms—starting at point A and moving from point to point along a fixed path to point Z. If this were a true depiction, we would be leaving early stages behind as we move forward, much as we leave Connecticut behind when we enter New York and leave New York behind as we enter New Jersey.

But this Hero's Journey is a process of spiritual growth, and it just doesn't work that way. We don't move from one linear point to another. We expand outward from our spiritual core. Each stage expands our old comfort zone as we experience increased faith in our Source and confidence in ourselves. We don't put down one archetype as we reach for another. Each archetype enlarges our sense of self and increases our strength as the journey unfolds.

This is precisely why the Bible is always a relevant and useful road map, no matter where we are on our journey. We never leave the Garden behind or Egypt or the wilderness. Every stage of the journey is still present within us. Those characters—those "thought people"—are still in our consciousness. They are less and less powerful as our understanding expands. But they're still there—especially the temptation to see ourselves as victims of powers beyond our control.

The whiny, "why-are-we-doing-this" energy of the Israelites in the wilderness is still very much with me. I move through it much more quickly now because it no longer represents the limits of my consciousness. I once could stretch a good fit of moping and pouting out for days, really reveling in my self-justified sense of being a pathetic victim. Today, if I try them on for size, moping and pouting quickly feel like the "things of a child" that I am only too eager to put away. But they're still there, lurking in consciousness. So reminders from Hebrew scripture about how vividly dualistic earlier stages can seem are very helpful in the course of any given day.

After all, even Jesus realized the negative energies trying to take advantage of his own time in the wilderness to twist his spiritual awakening to selfish ends would continue to be with him throughout his own journey. "Get behind me, Satan!" he tells his personal demons (Mt. 4:10). Not "Go away forever," or "Drop dead!" He knows better than to expect them to vanish. He just wants to be sure they're not in the driver's seat as his own Christ journey continues.

So it is entirely appropriate that pieces of the journey begin to reappear. It's also true that we are always engaged in multiple processes—journeys within journeys.

To take my good pal Harry Potter as an example; each of his seven years at Hogwarts is a complete Hero's Journey in itself—each brings him from Privet Lane and back again, transformed in the process by the year's adventures. At the same time, all seven years constitute a larger Hero's Journey of education and preparation. Those years are part of the even larger Hero's Journey of his entire life. At the other extreme, each day at Hogwarts is its own Hero's Journey, returning Harry at night to the bed he left in the morning having grown and learned from the events of the day.

It's the same for us. Something we learn on one journey may reappear as a reminder or insight on another. I really begin to think that there are no straight lines at all in the realm of spirit—only ever-expanding spirals of infinite possibility, carrying us around and around, but always upward. I'm sure the spiral will stop once we achieve kingdom consciousness, but will continue into infinity, carrying us to realms beyond our wildest imaginings.

At least, I hope so. I really can't see myself sitting around for all eternity with nothing creative or challenging to do. We are a creative spiritual energy that will always need to be creating.

MEDITATION

Centered and grateful, I wait with confidence for the smoke of negativity to clear in my consciousness, so that the Light can truly shine. Even when I cannot see, I sing the praises of the light I know is there.

Questions for Discussion

1. What type of music would be appropriate to the song lyric in this chapter? Lively? Solemn? Rhythmic? Calm? Why?

2. How do these angels seem or feel compared to the plague-bearing angels in earlier chapters? Have they changed? Have you?

3. Who is being kept out of the temple until the plagues have ended? Why?

4. Does this chapter about final challenges before a promised blessing remind you of anything from your own experience? What happened then?

Step 16

EMPTYING BOWLS OF WRATH

If any single chapter might cause us to give up entirely on the Revelation to John, this would probably be that chapter. The seven bowls of wrath, like the plagues we've already moved through, seem to be steeped in anger, judgment and unworthiness, designed to make us feel really, really bad about ourselves.

But remember, we're not condemned to live in these experiences. We're moving through them to release their power over us, because they cannot accompany us into the kingdom.

The bottom line is this: Even God cannot violate the Law that God is. The Law affirms that our choices have consequences. Because we are creative spiritual beings, we will—we must—experience the results of our choices. At this stage of spiritual awareness, we would not make the same choices we made earlier in the process. That's good. But it doesn't excuse us from the negative consequences we've been avoiding or denying as we moved along. They have to be faced so we can be freed of them. Their fearsome effects are never as bad as we expect them to be, and they are brief. The joyful freedom we feel in releasing them is more than we could have imagined, and it is eternal!

> "Then I heard a loud voice from the temple telling the seven angels, 'Go and pour out on the earth the seven bowls of the wrath of God.'"
>
> —Rev. 16:1

As we've already discussed, "the wrath of God" is really "the consequences of negative choices." God didn't make those choices, of course. We did. We do. Even this far into our spiritual journey, there are still thoughts in our consciousness that are rooted in old assumptions that the dualistic illusions of the two beasts are true. Many of our most obviously beast-related thoughts have been dissolved. Those that remain are far more subtle, so much a part of our consciousness that we don't even recognize them as distinct thoughts. They are simply "what we know" to be true. But as we have seen, "knowing what we know" can be our greatest spiritual impediment.

So the bowls of false belief must be emptied—not as punishment, but so we can be freed of their negative energies.

> "So the first angel went and poured his bowl on the earth, and a foul and painful sore came on those who had the mark of the beast and who worshiped its image."
>
> —Rev. 16:2

The seven plagues described here, like the seven trumpets of Chapters 8 and 9, are obviously intended to remind the reader of the plagues inflicted upon the people of Egypt in the Book of Exodus. But the difference between then and now is a measure of how far we've come in spiritual consciousness.

These plagues are not a punishment, nor the fulfillment of a divine threat. They are consequences of false beliefs and negative choices, experienced so we can free ourselves to move forward. We have long believed ourselves to be weak and vulnerable, victims of pain, injury and disease. Those beliefs are expressed here as painful sores. They are only felt by those thoughts still clinging to "the mark of the beast." We must always remember that those thoughts that are awake to our innate divinity are still gathered serenely by the lake of glass, observing and appreciating the cleansing process at work.

> "The second angel poured his bowl into the sea, and it became like the blood of a corpse, and every living thing in the sea died."
>
> —Rev. 16:3

The "blood of a corpse" is basically useless. It is stagnant and still. It no longer moves through the body, carrying the energy of life into every cell. This bowl contains the thoughts we still hold in consciousness insisting on the reality of death as the end of life. When these thoughts are poured out into the metaphysical sea—the realm of all possibility—they inevitably produce "after their kind" until their power is dissolved.

> "The third angel poured his bowl into the rivers and the springs of water, and they became blood. And I heard the angel of the waters say, 'You are just, O Holy One, who are and were, for you have judged these things; because they shed the blood of saints and prophets, you have given them blood to drink. It is what they deserve!' And I heard the altar respond, 'Yes, O Lord God, the Almighty, your judgments are true and just!'"
>
> —Rev. 16:4-7

The thoughts contained in the third bowl "become blood" in a different sense. These are the thoughts of judgment that refused to recognize the message of the "saints and prophets" who enter our lives as spiritual guides. We have "shed their blood" through our negative reactions to their loving efforts. We must now dissolve the power of those thoughts by "drinking the blood" of the saints and prophets—that is, by embracing their message and appreciating their work in our lives.

"Blood to drink" may sound punitive, but metaphysically it is just the opposite. It is empowering and life-enhancing, the gift of a loving divinity whose constant energy within us is, indeed, "true and just."

> "The fourth angel poured his bowl on the sun, and it was allowed to scorch them with fire; they were scorched by the fierce heat, but they cursed the name of God, who had authority over these plagues, and they did not repent and give him glory."
>
> —Rev. 16:8-9

From primitive beliefs to the more sophisticated religions of Egypt and Greece, the sun serves as a worldwide symbol for the light and power that is our eternal Source. The fourth bowl contains those thoughts that insist on seeing that Source as angry, destructive and punishing. That power of God only has "authority over these plagues" to the extent we use its Presence in us to create plagues. We must "repent"—rethink our relationship to the divine as one based in infinite love, not in anger. By affirming its glory, we replace plagues with infinite promise.

> "The fifth angel poured his bowl on the throne of the beast, and its kingdom was plunged into darkness; people gnawed their tongues in agony, and cursed the God of heaven because of their pains and sores, and they did not repent of their deeds."
>
> —Rev. 16:10-11

The fifth bowl contains all the thoughts (it must be an extra-large bowl) that insist on seeing us as victims—of God, of each other, of the world in general. Metaphysically, the divine idea of power is centered at the root of the tongue—because it is by "speaking the word" that our creative power is expressed. It is "agony" indeed to refuse to express that power; it requires us to resist our own creative nature, to be so addicted to the role of victim that we refuse to see ourselves any other way.

> "The sixth angel poured his bowl on the great river Euphrates, and its water was dried up in order to prepare the way for the kings from the east. And I saw three foul spirits like frogs coming from the mouth of the dragon, from the mouth of the beast, and from the mouth of the false prophet. These are demonic spirits, performing signs, who go abroad to the kings of the whole world, to assemble them for battle on the great day of God the Almighty. ('See, I am coming like a thief! Blessed is the one who stays awake and is clothed, not going about naked and exposed to shame.') And they assembled them at the place that in Hebrew is called Armageddon."
>
> —Rev. 16:12-16

We have previously referred to the Euphrates River—the eastern boundary of the Roman Empire—as the focus of great fear and many rumors. It was thought that someone—maybe the Parthians, maybe the not-really-dead Emperor Nero—was gathering massive armies intent on essentially destroying all of civilization. Today there are no places left on Earth unknown and mysterious enough to hide massive armies, so we tend to move such rumors into outer space and scare ourselves silly with tales of aliens from other worlds. Same difference.

The thoughts we are emptying here are those convinced that, in surrendering to our spiritual truth, we are making ourselves dangerously vulnerable to the "realities" of the world. "Let go and let God" is an easy buzz phrase but a truly frightening step to these thoughts insisting that we can't be too careful. "What if …" "Yes, but …" Our inner resistance is almost at an end; we're hanging on by our very fingertips to the illusive security of old beliefs.

The name *Armageddon* has been inflated through time into a one-word description of an ultimate, apocalyptic battle. The Hebrew term actually means "Hill of Megiddo." And Megiddo is the site of several important battles described in Hebrew scripture, involving Deborah (Judg. 5:19), Ahaziah (2 Kings 9:27) and Josiah (2 Chr. 35:22). The metaphysical implication, I think, is that while we have fought the same battle in consciousness many times before, it's time for a decisive victory.

> "The seventh angel poured his bowl into the air, and a loud voice came out of the temple, from the throne, saying, 'It is done!' And there came flashes of lightning, rumblings, peals of thunder, and a violent earthquake, such as had not occurred since people were upon the earth, so violent was that earthquake."

—Rev. 16:17-18

As we've discussed before, the Revelation to John is not presented in a clear, linear fashion; it offers a series of overlapping images that spiral around like a tornado, returning to the same spot again and again. This is even more apparent as we enter the final chapters. Instead of one definitive ending, we get a series of climactic moments, of which this is the first. "It is done!"

The final six chapters constitute a kind of "mopping up" process. It will involve more drama, but the outcome is certain. The seven bowls containing all the false thoughts and mistaken beliefs that provided a power base for the beast have been emptied. It wasn't a pretty process, but it's done. The imperfect world of dualistic illusion is shaken as never before—but not to worry! It is to be replaced with the new kingdom of heaven, anchored in spiritual truth.

> "The great city was split into three parts, and the cit-
> ies of the nations fell. God remembered great Babylon
> and gave her the wine-cup of the fury of his wrath.
> And every island fled away, and no mountains were to
> be found; and huge hailstones, each weighing about
> a hundred pounds, dropped from heaven on people,
> until they cursed God for the plague of the hail, so fear-
> ful was that plague."
>
> —Rev. 16:19-21

The "cities of the nations" represent the centers of mortal power, insisting on the reality of the dualistic illusion of life and death. As always in the Revelation to John, "Babylon" is a code name for Rome—the earlier conqueror of the Hebrew people equated with the oppression of the Roman Empire. The oppressors will find no refuge—islands will vanish and mountains will be leveled—and the consequence of both affirming the false and attacking the true will be severe indeed.

Thoughts on Step 16: Emptying Bowls of Wrath

For anyone who shares my grounding in the Twelve Steps of recovery from addictions, this vivid chapter—with all its blood and thunder—may seem vaguely familiar. I think it contains strong echoes of the Fourth Step: *Made a fearless and thorough moral inventory of ourselves.*

It's mildly embarrassing today to look back and realize how strenuously I resisted the Fourth Step in the early days of my recovery. Long after I had become willing to make new choices, to allow a spiritual dimension to tentatively surface in my life, I continued to ignore the advice of sponsors (not always gently given) that it was past time to focus on this step. Long after I had wandered through later steps, releasing and surrendering with wild enthusiasm, I assured myself that I had "kinda, sorta" done the Fourth by thinking about it every now and then.

I stayed sober. I went to many, many meetings. I shared my own story with others. I even sponsored a few newcomers (and, of course, urged them to do their own Fourth Step work). Life was certainly better than it had been. But something was missing; something was off. I moved through each day with a sense of angst and mild depression that prevented me from fully celebrating the new life unfolding through me.

I was living in Chicago by this time, about five years into the process of recovery. I was focused on a career as an actor and director, using office temp work to fill the gaps between theater projects. One unusual temp assignment put me in a completely empty law office after hours, from 6 to 11 p.m. My sole job was to listen to an apparently endless series of tapes. I didn't really need to hear what was said on the tapes; I just had to mark times at long intervals. I've forgotten what it was all about—or perhaps I never knew.

The boredom was nearly unbearable by the second week. But the money was good. I had time to contemplate the confusion of my life. It finally occurred to me that perhaps my spirit guides were fed up with my Fourth Step excuses. There I was, alone in an office for five hours a day, with an empty pad of paper and a supply of pens and pencils. Perhaps it was time to bite the bullet and write down the personal inventory I had so long resisted. And I did.

My Roman Catholic upbringing encouraged me to approach the Fourth Step as a kind of cosmic confession, in which I admitted my sins—which God already knew, of course, and had already entered into his record book. In this case, I was to admit all the terrible things I had done in the course of my addictive behavior in the hope that the admission would earn me at least a grudging energy of forgiveness. The Chapter 16 imagery of bowls of wrath is a pretty clear expression of the feeling I had as I began my far-from-fearless inventory.

But something totally unexpected happened as I devoted long hours to the process. Instead of the heavy sense of guilt with which I usually left the confessional, I was feeling increasingly light and incredibly free. I realized the sense of unworthiness I was describing in my inventory existed solely in my own mind. It consisted of all the negative energies my mortal consciousness used to keep me from embracing the full potential of my recovery—the full expression of my true Christ identity. I wasn't asking a distant, judgmental God to forgive me. I was choosing to forgive myself.

The same process is being described, I think, in the challenging images of this chapter. No one is more aware than I of just how undeserving I am for the kingdom of heaven, based on repressed memories of past choices and actions. My sponsor once told me, impatient with my endless angst, that the only problem I had with the Twelve Step program was that I was convinced I didn't deserve it. He was right. I have to clear out all that mental junk to make room for new energies of good. It's not a pretty process, but the result is more than worth it. I moved forward, forever changed. And so do we move forward in the Revelation, to the joyful promise of its final chapters.

MEDITATION

I AM eager to release old negative beliefs and memories that cannot continue with me as I continue my journey to the kingdom of heaven. I move fearlessly through the illusions of pain and confusion, confident that my journey is blessed and my way is clear.

Questions for Discussion

1. Can you think of an example from your own life of a painful process producing a positive and freeing outcome?

2. Was there more psychic pain in the process itself or in the fear that preceded it? What does that suggest about approaching similar processes in the future?

3. What are the negative connotations of being given "blood to drink"? Is there any way the image could be seen as a positive? If so, which choice seems more appropriate?

4. How does an accurate understanding of the term "Armageddon" affect your understanding of what the Revelation is describing?

Step 17

JUDGING THE GREAT WHORE

At the very outset of the Gospel of Thomas—the "fifth gospel," the text of which was found in the mid-1940s as a part of the Nag Hammadi discoveries in the Sinai Desert—Jesus provides us with a clear, succinct description of the spiritual process that will, nearly a century later, become the focus of the Revelation to John. "The seeker should not stop until he finds," he says in Logion Two. "When he does find, he will be disturbed. After having been disturbed, he will be astonished. Then he will reign over everything."

We move from "disturbed" to "astonished" in the course of Chapter 17. The process, just completed, of emptying the "bowls of wrath" has been challenging, confusing and, well, *disturbing*. The first consequence of that process is a new vision—a new way of seeing and comprehending the world. We are able to see beneath the surface of wealth, beauty and worldly success to the underlying negative energies of fear, judgment and greed. It isn't a pretty picture, but its clarity is amazing.

"Then one of the seven angels who had the seven bowls came and said to me, 'Come, I will show you the judgment of the great whore who is seated on many waters, with whom the kings of the earth have committed fornication, and with the wine of whose fornication the inhabitants of the earth have become drunk.' So he carried me away in the spirit into a wilderness, and I saw a woman sitting on a scarlet beast that was full of blasphemous names, and it had seven heads and ten horns. The woman was clothed in purple and scarlet, and adorned with gold and jewels and pearls, holding in her hand a golden cup full of abominations and the impurities of her fornication; and on her forehead was written a name, a mystery: 'Babylon the great, mother of whores and of earth's abominations.' And I saw that the woman was drunk with the blood of the saints and the blood of the witnesses to Jesus."

—Rev. 17:1-6

As I said, it's not a pretty picture! Freed from the seven bowls filled with the negative energies produced by our own mistaken choices, we are able to allow divine guidance to show us this human experience from a spiritual perspective. We see the dominant Roman Empire, not as a symbol of power, but as a "great whore" sitting upon the beast we first met in Chapter 13.

She is arrayed and adorned with gold and jewels, but there is nothing impressive or alluring about the image. We might once have been dazzled by her appearance or frightened by the power of the underlying beast. But with the clear-eyed vision we have newly achieved, we see her as repulsive, almost pathetic. We see her drunk on the blood of her victims, and we begin to realize for the first time that her apparent power over spiritual commitment is the ultimate lie.

We were once among those deluded beings eager to fornicate with the whore—to possess her and her riches for ourselves. We clearly see that she offers nothing we want; in this awareness, she ceases to be an impediment to our spiritual progress.

"When I saw her, I was greatly amazed. But the angel said to me, 'Why are you so amazed? I will tell you the mystery of the woman, and of the beast with seven heads and ten horns that carries her. The beast that you saw was, and is not, and is about to ascend from the bottomless pit and go to destruction. And the inhabitants of the earth, whose names have not been written in the book of life from the foundation of the world, will be amazed when they see the beast, because it was and is not and is to come.'"

—Rev. 17:6-8

Jesus said that following the disturbance of spiritual surrender comes astonishment; the Revelation uses the word *amazed*. What is it that is so astonishing, so amazing to our newly clear, freshly spiritualized sight? It is simply that the fear-based resistance to our spiritual awakening—the terrible beast, the overwhelming power of the world around us—is only an illusion, created and believed by the negative energies we have now released. All the fearful manifestations of punishment and resistance are easily dissolved in the light of spiritual awareness.

We saw in Chapter 3 that those "whose names have not been written in the book of life" are those who continue to believe in the illusion of death and the consciousness of limitation and fear it engenders. For them the beast "was and is not and is to come" because they continue to fear it, which gives it the only power it has. Like the feared and detested Emperor Nero, it will continue to threaten and terrorize those whose fear becomes a form of belief.

"This calls for a mind that has wisdom: the seven heads are seven mountains on which the woman is seated; also, they are seven kings, of whom five have fallen, one is living, and the other has not yet come; and when he comes, he must remain for only a little while. As for the beast that was and is not, it is an eighth but it belongs to the seven, and it goes to destruction. And the ten horns that you saw are ten kings who have not yet received a kingdom, but they are to receive authority as kings for one hour, together with the beast. These are united in yielding their power and authority to the beast; they will make war on the Lamb, and the Lamb will conquer them, for he is Lord of lords and King of kings, and those with him are called and chosen and faithful."

—Rev. 17:9-14

This guiding angel becomes the voice of our own indwelling divine guidance—and the mysteries that once baffled us are easily explained. As we have seen before, most of the specifics pertain to the time the Revelation was written. We can understand some of them—Rome is still a city noted for its seven hills, for example—but others, such as the specific kings referred to, are less clear.

The bottom line is that the worldly forces that depend on the beast for their power of negativity and fear "will make war" on the spiritual truth represented by the Lamb of God. This Lamb is the Christ—the gentle, loving divine energy that is our true self. It may seem feeble and weak against the fearful forces of the beast, but its power is always victorious when we call upon its Presence, choose to believe in its Truth, and remain unshaken in our commitment to our spiritual purpose.

"And he said to me, 'The waters that you saw, where the whore is seated, are peoples and multitudes and nations and languages. And the ten horns that you saw, they and the beast will hate the whore; they will make her desolate and naked; they will devour her flesh and burn her up with fire. For God has put it into their hearts to carry out his purpose by agreeing to give their kingdom to the beast, until the words of God will be fulfilled. The woman you saw is the great city that rules over the kings of the earth.'"

—Rev. 17:15-18

If we are astonished at the clarity with which we can now see the once-fearful powers of the world as a pathetic illusion, our astonishment will increase tenfold as our divine guidance continues to make clear what once seemed so confusing.

Why are these powers allowed to express? Why does God allow evil in the world? It's a question we come up against still today, on a regular basis. The astonishing answer echoes the insight Joseph has when his brothers plead for his forgiveness (Gen. 50:20): God meant it for good!

The conflict we have just experienced is not a punishment; it is not a sign of divine displeasure. It is the very essence of the creative process—the rhythm of divine energy eternally creating the new consciousness that is the "kingdom of heaven."

There is nothing to regret. There was no easier way that we missed or ignored. We are spiritual beings, here in human form precisely to face the beasts of duality and fear, to overcome their illusory power, and to contribute to the coming of the kingdom.

As was announced at the end of the previous chapter, "It is done!" There's nothing left but some quick mopping up, a well-earned celebration, and a prayerful, profoundly grateful appreciation of just what this new consciousness is that has been calling us forward through so much resistance.

Thoughts on Step 17: Judging the Great Whore

It's fairly short, and its imagery is pretty disgusting. Chapter 17 has certainly never been a favorite with those of the Revelation Fan Club who prefer predictions of personal punishment rather than explanations of the underlying structure of this human experience. But the more I work with it, the more I think that this may be the most important chapter of the entire Revelation.

We can easily set aside the specifics of the images described. The beast is, as it was when we first encountered it in Chapter Three, meant to embody the totality of the Roman Empire.

The great drunken whore represents the tangible allure of the Empire—its power, riches and sensual distractions.

It takes no great stretch of the imagination to apply the images to the political structure of the world today. Power in the hands of the spiritually ignorant is still an integral part of our experience; and it still engenders fear and dread.

At the same time, its negative energy continues to exert a strong fascination. To chase after sensual pleasure, worldly riches and some significant measure of the tangible power—to be part of the in crowd, successful and powerful in the eyes of the world—is no less seductive today, no matter what empire of false belief is holding sway in our consciousness.

None of us is immune to that temptation. Even Jesus, who came to perfectly embody the Christ Power that lives in each of us, was fully human, and therefore, fully susceptible to the lure of worldly pleasures. Some people wish we knew more about Jesus—what he was like, what made him laugh, what he really felt about the pressures and demands of his ministry. I can understand this desire to know more about his specific human personality. But I also think you can learn a lot about an individual if you know something about what tempts him—what particular expressions of sensual pleasure he finds it hardest to resist.

In the synoptic Gospels of Mark, Matthew and Luke, Jesus is baptized by John the Baptist at the beginning of his public ministry and immediately goes off into the wilderness, on a sort of vision quest. The baptism had symbolically awakened him to his spiritual power, and he had to decide what to do with this profound, new awareness. He encounters his own ego self in the wilderness, conveniently represented in the Gospels as a tangible demon. The ego message is clear and seductive: You can use this newfound power to achieve lots of worldly goodies.

Now, temptation is a very personal thing; what tempts you may have no appeal to me at all, and vice versa. And each of us

| Kingdom Come

has a demon—an ego self—that is completely aware of what our personal weak spots might be. So I think we learn a lot about Jesus the man by noticing just what it is he finds most tempting.

It's not sex, or chocolate, or the winning lottery numbers every week—as it might be for any of us. No, what his personal demon recognizes is a hunger for security ("You can turn these stones into bread and never be hungry again"), fame ("Throw yourself off the temple, let angels catch you, and see how much attention you'll attract") and, most seductive of all, the absolute power to rule the world and force it to fall into line.

It's only when he realizes that even well-intended temporal power is a spiritual trap that Jesus is free to commit his Christ energy to teaching and demonstrating spiritual principle among the people with whom he is interacting daily. The temptations don't vanish, of course; he's still engaged in a human experience. He will encounter them again and again as his ministry unfolds. After the initial choice in the wilderness, it becomes easier to make the consistently efficient choice—to keep the ego out of the driver's seat, even though it's still going to be along for the ride.

All of us, once we awaken to our true spiritual identity, are presented with the same challenge, over and over again. We must continually choose whether to place our faith and focus on the attractions of this dualistic experience, or whether to dismiss the attractions and hold firm to our spiritual purpose.

I feel safe in saying that none of us opts for the spiritual in the face of every temptation. Because we are now awake, aware of the choices before us and the implications of each, we can be extremely hard on ourselves for failing to choose perfectly.

When our inner guidance carries us off to our own wilderness experience in this chapter, it is for a very different reason. We don't simply need to affirm our spiritual purpose; we also need to forgive our human failings.

So, along with a vivid depiction of the human condition—addicted, distracted, in thrall to false beliefs and negative energy, deceived by false prophets and ignorant of our own greatness—comes the simple, shocking teaching we most need to hear. God means it all for good. There is nothing to fear because there is nothing that is not God. There is nothing to feel shame about because God was in every option of every choice we've ever faced. The fact that we've made it this far, that we're able to see the human from the perspective of the divine, means that no matter how painful, confused, lonely or fearful we have felt as a result of some choices, we have succeeded in releasing the divine potential in each and all of them.

Could we have chosen paths that were easier, more direct and more loving? Probably. But that wouldn't necessarily have been a good thing. Jesus emphasized that it's the wide path—the path of the sleepwalkers—that is the easiest choice. We are not here in human form to always make the easiest choice. It is precisely through our wide-awake encounters with the gaudy demons and fearful beasts of our human illusions that we transform them into aspects of the divine. That's our entire purpose for being here at all.

The final chapters of the Revelation to John celebrate and appreciate the end of one particular cycle of the Hero's Journey that is our spiritual purpose. We saw in the last step that we're already starting to feel called to other journeys still to come. Nothing is more essential as we continue forward than that we remove from our consciousness the superstitious insistence that we're supposed to do it perfectly, and every instance of misguided choice should be a cause of guilt and shame.

We cleared that all out with the seven bowls of Chapter 16. The next journey will be infinitely easier if we learn the great lesson of Chapter 17, and resist the urge to start accumulating a fresh supply of shameful secrets and relentless guilt.

MEDITATION

I move through this and every day focused on my spiritual path and purpose. I embrace every expression of shadow and light without fear or shame, for they are all essential to my creative work.

Questions for Discussion

1. How does the imagery of this chapter make you feel? Why?
2. Do you think there's a positive reason for the emphasis on negative appearances?
3. What is the overreaching message this chapter's vision is meant to communicate?
4. Can you think of an apparently negative choice or experience in your past that might appear in a different light from the perspective of this vision?

Step 18

GRIEVING THE OLD

The prophetic books of Isaiah, Jeremiah and Ezekiel in Hebrew Scripture all contain examples of a verse form known as a "taunt song." It's basically a form of literary gloating. The closest equivalent in English is probably "nana nana na na," although it really takes the requisite tonality to get the point across.

At any rate, Chapter 18 offers the only example of a taunt song in the New Testament. Today we would probably consider it a form of poor sportsmanship. But given the drama we've just been through in the first 17 chapters, a little gloating over our spiritual triumph doesn't seem out of order—especially when angels are doing the taunting.

> "After this I saw another angel coming down from heaven, having great authority; and the earth was made bright with his splendor. He called out with a mighty voice, 'Fallen, fallen is Babylon the great! It has become a dwelling place of demons, a haunt of every foul and hateful bird, a haunt of every foul and hateful beast. For all the nations have drunk of the wine of the wrath of her fornication, and the kings of the earth have committed fornication with her, and the merchants of the earth have grown rich from the power of her luxury.'"

—Rev. 18:1-3

As always in the Revelation to John, we understand Babylon to represent Rome. (Probably writing "Fallen, fallen is Rome the great!" would not have been a politically safe idea.) Again as always, we understand Rome to be a metaphysical image of the dualistic ego consciousness, with its belief in lack, punishment, guilt and other apparently negative energies.

It is this limitation consciousness, heavily vested in affirming the reality of our human suffering that has been our constant adversary throughout our journey. It is still present—it will continue to be with us as long as we continue our mortal experience—but from our new spiritual perspective, it's hard to believe it ever held any appeal. We can now see it for what it is—a "haunt" for every expression of negate emotions, hateful ideas and self-centered greed that has evolved through our previous ignorance of spiritual possibility.

> "Then I heard another voice from heaven saying, 'Come out of her, my people,so that you do not take part in her sins, and so that you do not share in her plagues; for her sins are heaped high as heaven, and God has remembered her iniquities. Render to her as she herself has rendered, and repay her double for her deeds; mix a double draught for her in the cup she mixed. As she glorified herself and lived luxuriously, so give her a like measure of torment and grief.'"

—Rev. 18:4-7

Even in the midst of our celebration, we must be careful not to fall once again into the trap of duality. Babylon/Rome/ego consciousness is not a power opposite to God. Those thoughts in consciousness still caught in the illusion are simply vestiges of our previous ignorance.

I feel a great love in the invitation to "Come out of her, my people." We once believed ourselves trapped in the negative, a victim of forces beyond our control. Now—and from here on out—we will be using a power of choice we didn't know we had to withdraw our thoughts and attitudes from Babylon and place them instead in the kingdom to come.

It's also important to note that, now that we have awakened and successively completed one Hero's Journey of spiritual realization, there is a price to pay in consciousness. We can no longer hide behind the excuse of powerlessness. We know better; we know the creative power expressing through us. Therefore, the consequences of negative choices will be even greater than in the past. We will receive a "double draught" of consequence for each fear-based choice we make …

> "Since in her heart she says, 'I rule as a queen; I am no widow, and I will never see grief,' therefore her plagues will come in a single day—pestilence and mourning and famine—and she will be burned with fire; for mighty is the Lord God who judges her."
>
> —Rev. 18:7-8

I have heard many people comment in recent years that there seems to be a significant speed-up in experiencing the consequences of our choices—positive or negative. Choices have always had consequences, of course; but the space of time between choice and consequence is continually shortening once we recognize the truth of our creative power.

This passage is also an example of how subtle inflections in meaning can be an expression of the translator's innate assumptions. The word translated as "judges" does not carry with it the full implications of the English. There is no punishment imposed by a vengeful Lord God; there is simply the expression of Divine Law.

"And the kings of the earth, who committed fornication and lived in luxury with her, will weep and wail
over her when they see the smoke of her burning;
they will stand far off, in fear of her torment, and say,
'Alas, alas, the great city, Babylon, the mighty city!
For in one hour your judgment has come.'"

—Rev. 18:9-10

The consequences of our successful journey are more
far-reaching than we might ever have imagined, and it's important we understand the transformative energy we now express is
being felt in places far beyond our limited lives.

Why do we need to know this? Because the journeys still
to come will be easier to accomplish once we understand how
highly important and far-reaching our spiritual choices are felt.

"And the merchants of the earth weep and mourn for
her, since no one buys their cargo anymore, cargo of
gold, silver, jewels and pearls, fine linen, purple, silk
and scarlet, all kinds of scented wood, all articles of
ivory, all articles of costly wood, bronze, iron, and mar-
ble, cinnamon, spice, incense, myrrh, frankincense,
wine, olive oil, choice flour and wheat, cattle and
sheep, horses and chariots, slaves—and human lives.
'The fruit for which your soul longed has gone from
you, and all your dainties and your splendor are lost to
you, never to be found again!' The merchants of these
wares, who gained wealth from her, will stand far off,
in fear of her torment, weeping and mourning aloud,
'Alas, alas, the great city, clothed in fine linen, in purple
and scarlet, adorned with gold, with jewels, and with
pearls! For in one hour all this wealth has been laid
waste!'"

—Rev. 18:11-17

Passages such as this provide a smug sense of self-satisfaction when applied to the material world in which we live—as Revelation enthusiasts have been doing for 2,000 years, seeing in every economic crisis a sign that the final days are at hand. They've been consistently wrong so far. It's only when we turn within, and recognize the thoughts, fears and feelings in our own consciousness that have been heavily invested in the illusion of duality, that we receive the useful lesson that even in times of spiritual accomplishment, there is a significant energy within us that is grieving the past.

> "And all shipmasters and seafarers, sailors and all whose trade is on the sea, stood far off and cried out as they saw the smoke of her burning, 'What city was like the great city?' And they threw dust on their heads, as they wept and mourned, crying out, 'Alas, alas, the great city, where all who had ships at sea grew rich by her wealth! For in one hour she has been laid waste.'"
> —Rev. 18:17-19

And the grieving continues, even in the parts of consciousness that were not deeply invested in the "great city" of old limitations. It is important to recognize that no matter how excited we are to leave a comfort zone that no longer comforts, there will be a grieving process to move through.

We often assume we should be feeling nothing but joy. We wonder what's wrong with us. We try to hide the grief behind a grinning façade. The simple truth is, grieving is natural and inevitable. The more easily we acknowledge it, the more quickly it dissolves.

> "Rejoice over her, O heaven, you saints and apostles and prophets! For God has given judgment for you against her.

Then a mighty angel took up a stone like a great millstone and threw it into the sea, saying, 'With such violence Babylon the great city will be thrown down, and will be found no more; and the sound of harpists and minstrels and of flutists and trumpeters will be heard in you no more; and an artisan of any trade will be found in you no more; and the sound of the millstone will be heard in you no more; and the light of a lamp will shine in you no more; and the voice of bridegroom and bride will be heard in you no more; for your merchants were the magnates of the earth, and all nations were deceived by your sorcery. And in you was found the blood of prophets and of saints, and of all who have been slaughtered on earth.'"

—Rev. 18:20-24

While we are caught up in the drama and conflict of a spiritual Hero's Journey, it often seems that its purpose is simply survival. On a better day, we might allow ourselves the slightest of hopes that we might be accomplishing something of lasting battle—but never do we fully comprehend the universal implications of what we're doing.

There's a danger that even the successful completion of a journey might seem like no big deal. So it's very important that we pause to hear this song of amazing consequences—to realize that nothing will ever be the same.

In our earlier stages of ignorance, we often were able to bring sparks of accidental light to the darkness of Babylon. No more. We are now in a state of consciousness in which negative beliefs manifest immediately as negative consequences. It's like the ruins of a once-powerful city that is nothing more than a shadow of itself. To return to it now would be to live in a cemetery of old values, trying to pretend they still had relevance or meaning.

Thoughts on Step 18: Grieving the Old

At about the four-year mark of my involvement with the Twelve Step program of Alcoholics Anonymous, I attended a weekend AA conference with an extensive selection of relevant discussions. I forget what workshop I wanted to attend, but I found myself in the wrong room. It was a crowded room, however, and I was stuck back in the corner farthest from the door. The presenter had already started to speak by the time I realized my mistake, and I felt I had no choice but to stay where I was.

Now, I know many of you have already raised at least one eyebrow, or perhaps allowed yourself a slightly smug smile. There is no "'wrong" room, and we always have a choice. Clearly divine guidance was at work; I can see that now, but it was far from obvious at the time.

The topic of the wrong workshop was "Grieving." I knew it was going to be a waste of my time, because I wasn't grieving. My parents were both still alive at that time; I had not yet experienced the loss of friends. Grieving had nothing to do with me.

I was dissolved in tears by the end of the workshop, blubbering uncontrollably, releasing feelings I had been ignoring for years. It wasn't that I had deliberately repressed an inner feeling of grief; I simply had no clue it was even there! I hadn't recognized the human tendency to grieve over every change, every step into the unknown.

Surrendering to my addictive powerlessness is still today the most significant choice I have ever made, and even all those years ago, I felt deeply grateful for the Higher Power within me that was accomplishing what I could never have achieved with my limited human consciousness.

But, geez, talk about grief! An entire identity had died within me, and a whole range of thoughts and feelings were totally lost and adrift.

I have already mentioned the truism that "AA really screws up your drinking," meaning that once you have realized you are responsible for the choices you make, you can no longer hide in the pretense of simply being a victim. You may decide to return to the addiction, but you will always know you have made that choice. The realization that there is no going back was, I think, the hidden source of much of my unexplored grief.

To add to the grieving, I had very recently quit smoking! Cigarettes had been my constant companion for years—a protective fire between me and the rest of the world, an image of social poise, something to do when nothing else came to mind. I was happy to be free of their negative energy. But it would have been foolhardy not to realize that I was also grieving them deeply.

I remember that "wrong workshop" experience when I read the taunt song of Chapter 18. We have every reason to celebrate a victory over negative energies and fear-based beliefs. But, as the two angel guides make clear, it's also important to realize there will be an inevitable grieving process involved with even the most glorious spiritual realization. We can't safely ignore it, and we shouldn't resist it, or feel ashamed because our thoughts and feelings are not unanimous in their appreciation of what has happened.

Babylon the great has indeed fallen—and that's the best possible news. Unfortunately, we spent a lot of time in the dark alley and murky byways of that fear-based city. It was scary and painful, but it was familiar. Grieving is an essential part of the process of releasing ourselves from its shadowy grip.

MEDITATION

Today I give thanks that I am free of the fallen city filled with fear, lack and negative beliefs through which I have traveled on my spiritual path. At the same time I recognize a sense of grief as I leave behind me elements of the city that have long represented a comfort zone for me. I take much light and love with me as I leave the city. I allow my grief to dissolve in the promise of greater joy as I continue my journey.

Questions for Discussion

1. How do you relate this "taunt song" to your own journey? What does Babylon represent in your own past?

2. "Come out of her, my people" suggests that while the city represents negative energy, it also contains positive elements worth saving. How does that pertain to your own Babylon?

3. In what way has grieving been a part of your spiritual path? How does recognizing grief for what it is help the process of moving forward?

Step 19

AFFIRMING THE NEW

We have exulted over our spiritual victory in the preceding chapter, while at the same time remembering there is good to be claimed and embraced in the ruins of the fallen city. It's not time to affirm that the victory is not ours alone. We can only receive the full blessings of our new consciousness when we are centered in a grateful awareness of God as the Source of our strength, guidance and success.

> "After this I heard what seemed to be the loud voice of a great multitude in heaven, saying, 'Hallelujah! Salvation and glory and power to our God, for his judgments are true and just; he has judged the great whore who corrupted the earth with her fornication, and he has avenged on her the blood of his servants.' Once more they said, 'Hallelujah! The smoke goes up from her forever and ever.' And the twenty-four elders and the four living creatures fell down and worshiped God who is seated on the throne, saying, 'Amen. Hallelujah!'"
>
> —Rev. 19:1-4

We are back in the throne room of God, to which we were first lifted in Chapter 4. The scene and the cast of characters are the same, but the tone is quite different. Instead of concern that the seven seals could not be opened, the multitude of voices sing in praise of the great victory and its source in the "salvation and glory and power" of the divine.

The smoke going up "forever and ever" reassures us that the victory is both complete and permanent; this particular "great whore" will not have to be faced again.

The 24 elders again represent the 12 tribes of Israel and the 12 disciples of Jesus—the underlying structure of traditional religion for those Jews and Christians to whom the Revelation is addressed. The four living creatures—lion, ox, human and eagle—are symbols of human and animal life forms in our mortal experience. They were not able to achieve the victory on their own; they needed "the Lamb"—our own awareness and expression of our innate Christ nature—to accomplish this spiritual progress.

> "And from the throne came a voice saying, 'Praise our God, all you his servants, and all who fear him, small and great.'"
>
> —Rev. 19:5

At this point the triumphant celebration begins to take on the trappings of a religious liturgy, with the celebrant calling for prayers of praise and thanksgiving. We have seen earlier that the emotional resonance of the word translated as "fear" is actually closer to what we might call "awe." There is nothing to fear from our divine Source, but we must stand in awe of the power and potential of its Presence.

> "Then I heard what seemed to be the voice of a great multitude, like the sound of many waters and like the sound of mighty thunderpeals, crying out, 'Hallelujah! For the Lord our God the Almighty reigns. Let us rejoice and exult and give him the glory, for the marriage of the Lamb has come, and his bride has made herself ready; to her it has been granted

> to be clothed with fine linen, bright and pure' —
> for the fine linen is the righteous deeds of the saints."

—Rev. 19:6-8

The nature of the sacred liturgy now becomes even clearer. It is a wedding. In fact, it is *our* wedding, the marriage in each of us of the spiritual and the mortal.

In Jewish belief, it was only in the innermost depths of the Temple in Jerusalem—the Holy of Holies—that God and man came into direct connection. To some Christians that meeting place exists only in the person of Jesus Christ. To Jesus himself, however, each of us is a temple of God; it is within each of us that the divine and the human come together.

As Paul writes to the church in Corinth (1 Cor. 3:16): "Do you not know that you are God's temple and that God's Spirit dwells in you?"

Similarly, Jewish prophets use the image of a marriage to describe the desired union of God with the people of Israel. In the light of Christ understanding, each of us is individually called to "make ourselves ready" as the bride, clothed in the fine linen of positive faith and right action. It is, in fact, our mortal self—freed from the stain of negative energies—that is now ready to merge intimately with the Christ of our being.

> "And the angel said to me, 'Write this: Blessed are those who are invited to the marriage supper of the Lamb.' And he said to me, 'These are true words of God.' Then I fell down at his feet to worship him, but he said to me, 'You must not do that! I am a fellow servant with you and your comrades who hold the testimony of Jesus. Worship God! For the testimony of Jesus is the spirit of prophecy.'"

—Rev. 19:9-10

Do not worship the messenger! Focus instead on the Source. This is an urgent and timely lesson for each of us as we evaluate what we've learned in the course of the spiritual journey described in the Revelation.

Just as the early Israelites insisted on giving away a portion of their personal power to someone serving as their king, so do we today often give away spiritual power to a specific teacher, book, belief or tradition. It was a bad idea then, and it's a bad idea now.

Our marriage commitment is not to any intermediate messenger, but to the Presence of God Itself. The messenger may well be speaking the truth, as this angel obviously was. Nonetheless, "the testimony of Jesus" calls us to worship only the Source, not the channels through which it flows to us.

> "Then I saw heaven opened, and there was a white horse! Its rider is called Faithful and True, and in righteousness he judges and makes war. His eyes are like a flame of fire, and on his head are many diadems; and he has a name inscribed that no one knows but himself. He is clothed in a robe dipped in blood, and his name is called The Word of God. And the armies of heaven, wearing fine linen, white and pure, were following him on white horses. From his mouth comes a sharp sword with which to strike down the nations, and he will rule them with a rod of iron; he will tread the winepress of the fury of the wrath of God the Almighty. On his robe and on his thigh he has a name inscribed, 'King of kings and Lord of lords.'"

—Rev. 19:11-16

Okay, here comes the groom! What an entrance it is! We last saw the Christ in Chapter 6, emerging from the great scroll in response to the opening of the first seal. At that time, he had no real image or identity; we were more aware of his white horse than of the rider as he rode out and disappeared over the horizon without a word.

The Christ was only a potential then—a promise of future transformation we were not yet ready to fully grasp. He has now become a magnificent figure, but still mysterious. He alone knows who he really is, but "the testimony of Jesus" assures us that he is, in fact, us.

"In the beginning was the Word," according to the Gospel of John (1:1). And here, at the dramatic climax, not just of the Revelation to John, but of the entire Bible, it is once again the creative Power of the Word that is to be married to our human personality. It is as strong, specific and powerful as a sword, this Word of God that creates according to our faith and commitment.

> "Then I saw an angel standing in the sun, and with a loud voice he called to all the birds that fly in midheaven, 'Come, gather for the great supper of God, to eat the flesh of kings, the flesh of captains, the flesh of the mighty, the flesh of horses and their riders—flesh of all, both free and slave, both small and great.' Then I saw the beast and the kings of the earth with their armies gathered to make war against the rider on the horse and against his army. And the beast was captured, and with it the false prophet who had performed in its presence the signs by which he deceived those who had received the mark of the beast and those who worshiped its image. These two were thrown alive into the lake of fire that burns with sulfur. And the rest were killed by the sword of the rider on the horse, the sword that came from his mouth; and all the birds were gorged with their flesh."
>
> —Rev. 19:17-21

After 18 vivid chapters of suffering, fear, anticipation and preparation, the great, decisive battle could not be more of an anticlimax. Isn't that so often true in our own lives as well? We suffer great anguish from fearing a battle, or agonizing about it, or trying to anticipate what it will be like and preparing ourselves for the worst. Then, when the conflict finally arrives, it's over before we can even register its presence, and we're left to wonder what we had been so worked up about.

Once we are ready to call forth the Christ, the battle is essentially over. Yes, "the beast and the kings of the earth" gather and try to resist this new spiritual energy, but they are effortlessly conquered.

The two beasts (12:18-13:18; the second beast here is dubbed "the false prophet" of misguided religious belief) are not destroyed. They are thrown into the "lake of fire" so impurities of negativity can be burned away, and the energy that remains can transform into an expression of truth.

The kings and armies that supported the beasts are destroyed by the creative power of the Word—the sword that came from the mouth of the Christ. Anytime we speak spiritual Truth to appearances of mortal power, we may be sure Truth will easily conquer.

It's worth noting, too, that the Power of God is nothing if not efficient. Not a thing is wasted. The stagnant energy of negative thoughts becomes food for a new and free-flowing dimension of spiritual ideas and deeper understanding.

Thoughts on Step 19: Affirming the New

William Blake, the great English poet, printmaker and spiritual mystic, titled one of his most enduring works *The Marriage of Heaven and Hell.* He saw this union as not only desirable, but essential to our collective spiritual process. "Without contraries is no progression," he wrote. "Attraction and repulsion, reason and energy, love and hate, are necessary to human existence. From these contraries spring what the religious call Good and Evil. Good is the passive that obeys reason. Evil is the active, springing from energy."

The Revelation to John does not identify the bride and groom in this chapter as heaven and hell, but I think the energies involved are identical to Blake's understanding. According to the explanation of Jesus' teachings set forth in the Gospel of Philip (another Nag Hammadi find), we are not only both the groom and the bride; we are also the bridal chamber.

Like the Temple of Hebrew tradition, the bridal chamber is meant to allow for a union of "contraries"—male and female, spiritual and mortal. As Blake notes, "the religious" add a dimension of judgment and label the contraries as good and evil.

At best, a marriage of good and evil would produce only a lukewarm sort of middle ground that is neither. Such a tepid consciousness can hardly be the purpose of this great Hero's Journey that occupies our energies once we allow ourselves to be nudged beyond our first comfort zone.

If God is all Good, and God is everywhere present, then we must be experiencing a marriage of two distinct expressions of Good. Nothing else is possible. So the long religious tradition— by no means unique to Christianity—that insists on seeing this world as inherently evil, to be shunned in all possible ways, cannot lead us to the union of human and divine that is meant to occur in the spiritual bridal chamber of Jesus' teaching and Blake's vision.

The blink-and-you'll-miss-it battle that finally occurs in this chapter is actually the culmination of a long and challenging sort of military campaign that has carried us through many trials and adventures. We've had to move out of cherished old comfort zones, admit and release the dimensions of spiritual ignorance in which we had been existing, and surrender to an unknown Power of Infinite Love that forces us to see everything through new eyes. It's not surprising that we find ourselves tempted to return to a dualistic perspective and celebrate a victory over "the bad guys."

That's why this chapter is so perceptive, and so important. A bridal chamber is not a battlefield. (I'll now pause briefly for the cynical jokes and wisecracks.) One is about claiming victory; the other is about finding and expressing a deep spiritual union. The only battle necessary is against those aspects of consciousness that resist the idea of spiritual union—and even those aspects are not destroyed, but purified and returned to spiritual Source so they can eventually express in ways supportive of that union.

An important element of the promises associated with the Twelve Steps of recovery is that "We will not regret the past, nor wish to shut the door on it." Sometimes—particularly in the midst of a particularly rewarding ministerial experience—I find myself beset with thoughts of regret. If only I hadn't wasted so many years wallowing in my addictions. If only my "call to ministry" had come at an earlier time in my life. The imagery of this chapter helps me to stay centered, to realize the confusion of those "wasted" years is, in fact, an integral part of my sense of ministry today.

Whatever we may have done battle against—and no matter what battles may lie ahead—it's all Good! It may not always be nice, but it's always Good.

We were misguided in the past, when we decided to choose the demands of this human experience over the promise of spiritual Truth. We would be equally misguided today if we were to decide to choose spiritual Truth over the human experience.

We were fully spirit before we assumed these human earth suits, and we'll be fully spirit when we decide to put them down and move on. The whole point of being here now is to be the bridal chamber in which the pure energy of Spirit interacts intimately with the denser fog of physicality, creating a new consciousness that is not half one and half the other, but fully and completely both.

MEDITATION

I AM a witness for the marriage in my consciousness of the creative power of the divine and the creative opportunities of this human experience. I choose to live my life as a sacred expression of the kingdom of heaven that is conceived and birthed in me.

Questions for Discussion

1. How does the "throne room of God" feel to you now? Has that feeling changed since Chapter Four? If so, how? What might that change suggest?

2. There is more to the idea of "marriage" than simply the joining of two forces. There is an intimate, sensual experience of love given and received. How comfortable (or not) does that imagery feel? What does it suggest about the relationship between our Christ selves and our mortal personalities?

3. Why do you think the energy of the Christ is absent for so long, when we could certainly have used it in our battles with the two beasts? Is it really absent? Why does it suddenly appear now?

Step 20

DISCERNING CONSEQUENCES

I mentioned in the introduction to this book the popular *Left Behind* series of novels by Tim LaHaye and Jerry Jenkins, who approach the Revelation to John very literally and imagine how it might play out in the contemporary world. Much of the imagery they use comes from this chapter, which describes the immediate and future consequences of the victory described in Chapter 19.

Does their apocalyptic vision accurately express the energy of this chapter? Is there a real danger that a sudden "Rapture" might carry off, say, an airline pilot in mid-flight? Should we play it safe and fly only with pilots whose lives are so sinful there's no chance they'll qualify for the Rapture? Stay tuned!

> "Then I saw an angel coming down from heaven, holding in his hand the key to the bottomless pit and a great chain. He seized the dragon, that ancient serpent, who is the Devil and Satan, and bound him for a thousand years, and threw him into the pit, and locked and sealed it over him, so that he would deceive the nations no more, until the thousand years were ended. After that he must be let out for a little while."

—Rev. 20:1-3

Nothing could be more foolish than to assume human measurements of the phenomenon we call "time" have any relevance in the realm of Spirit. As the psalmist observes of God in Psalm 90, "A thousand years in your sight are like yesterday when it is past, or like a watch in the night." Satan—"that ancient serpent"—is a symbolic manifestation of our own fears and false beliefs. It is as a consequence of the journey we are completing that its power can now be locked away as we focus on the rich and wonderful possibilities of the new dimension of consciousness we've reached.

The fact that Satan still exists means there are still negative thoughts and false beliefs in our collective consciousness—he wouldn't be here otherwise. At some point, as our understanding continues to grow and deepen, we're going to have to deal with those remnants of the once-powerful dragon.

After all the work we've already done, there is clearly no danger left—just some cleanup work requiring us to apply our new understanding to the thoughts still hiding deep in consciousness. It sounds like walking a somewhat unruly dog—it just takes *"a little while."*

> "Then I saw thrones, and those seated on them were given authority to judge. I also saw the souls of those who had been beheaded for their testimony to Jesus and for the word of God. They had not worshiped the beast or its image and had not received its mark on their foreheads or their hands. They came to life and reigned with Christ for a thousand years. (The rest of the dead did not come to life until the thousand years were ended.) This is the first resurrection. Blessed and holy are those who share in the first resurrection. Over these the second death has no power, but they will be priests of God and of Christ, and they will reign with him for a thousand years."

—Rev. 20:4-6

The earliest followers of Jesus Christ expected him to return very quickly—certainly within their lifetimes. When years passed and that didn't happen, there was tremendous concern about those people who were dying off, especially those who were being put to death for their faith. That concern is addressed here with the promise that they get to go first! Theirs will be the "first resurrection."

Later biblical fundamentalists expanded the concept of the first resurrection to include all those who lead perfect lives, without worshipping the beast or receiving its mark. This has come to be known as the Rapture, or as Christian Millennialism.

They will be carried off to reign with Christ for a thousand years, while the rest of us (I have no hope of being included in the first resurrection) continue to suffer here below. You can decide for yourself what this passage means. I would only point out that I can find no suggestion that this first resurrection involves being taken away from the earth to someplace higher and better. The assumption seems to be that it happens right here.

Metaphysically, we understand the martyrs initially included in this first resurrection represent those thoughts in our own consciousness that have "held the high watch," never buying into the illusion of duality. It seems only reasonable that those thoughts, beliefs and understanding will be immediately absorbed into the new dimension of Spirit that is our Christ reality. So the coming of the kingdom of heaven is not a sudden event but a progression involving several stages of spiritual awareness and expression.

> "When the thousand years are ended, Satan will be released from his prison and will come out to deceive the nations at the four corners of the earth, Gog and Magog, in order to gather them for battle; they are as numerous as the sands of the sea. They marched up over the breadth of the earth and surrounded the camp of the saints and the beloved city. And fire came down

from heaven and consumed them. And the devil who had deceived them was thrown into the lake of fire and sulfur, where the beast and the false prophet were, and they will be tormented day and night forever and ever."

—Rev. 20:7-10

Let's break this down as best we can, to make sense out of what seems to be a very confusing passage. First of all, "Gog and Magog" is a deliberate echo of the prophet Ezekiel at his most apocalyptic (Ezek. 38 and 39). The prophet uses Gog, king of the tribe of Magog, to symbolize the threat he sees looming from Babylon. Magog is listed in Genesis (10:2) as a descendent of Japheth, son of Noah, who leaves the ark to populate the land to the north—Asia Minor at the time of the Revelation, the nation of Turkey today. In Ezekiel, the terms are used to vaguely define an unknown threat from an unknown enemy, located somewhere to the north.

While these details are academically helpful, they don't provide the metaphysical dimension we need to really claim the meaning of this passage. For that, as always, we have to turn within and recognize these combative forces in our own consciousness. I find it reassuring that we're not to expect a single, decisive victory—neat, clean and absolute. Overcoming negative energy is a process, not a single battle. We live in the process until, when it is appropriate in divine time, the remnant of Satan consciousness we have locked within ourselves will be freed so it can be properly and permanently dissolved.

It may gather some illusive strength from vague thoughts and fears that have not been transformed in the "first resurrection." These insistently dark and negative thoughts will surround "the beloved city," but they will be quickly dissolved by the power of divine Light.

This beloved city, about which we are going to read much more, is simply an image of the Christ Light of our own being.

Once we are established in its energy, we can safely face any negative fears and beliefs hiding in the shadows of our consciousness; we know that by claiming our innate Oneness with the infinite Good that is God, we remain centered. Satan consciousness will certainly reappear from time to time, but the holy city within us is impervious to its seductive voice and illusory distractions.

So now Satan, the great and ancient dragon given life by the choices we have made to empower its negative beliefs and false idols, can no longer survive without our continuing belief in its power. Into the lake of fire it goes, along with the great beasts of worldly power and religious deception.

Remember that this lake is a part of the energy of God—everything is—and thus an essential part of the creative process that is bringing the kingdom into expression. In fact, the torments described can best be understood as residual fears of separation from God. It suggests to me that while we can fully access our Christ Power while still living a dualistic human life, there will always be shadow thoughts and old fears clinging to a sense of separation until it is time to shrug off our earth suits and return entirely to the realm of Spirit.

> "Then I saw a great white throne and the one who sat on it; the earth and the heaven fled from his presence, and no place was found for them."
>
> —Rev. 20:11

This is the very pinnacle of spiritual unity. It's not that the earth disappears and we find ourselves in heaven. It's rather than both heaven and earth vanish as separate ideas, and we are left alone with God, radiant in the truth of our eternal Oneness.

> "And I saw the dead, great and small, standing before the throne, and books were opened. Also another

book was opened, the book of life. And the dead were judged according to their works, as recorded in the books. And the sea gave up the dead that were in it, Death and Hades gave up the dead that were in them, and all were judged according to what they had done. Then Death and Hades were thrown into the lake of fire. This is the second death, the lake of fire; and anyone whose name was not found written in the book of life was thrown into the lake of fire."

—Rev. 20:12-15

Judgment is one of the most paradoxical of spiritual concepts. On one hand, it is one of our Twelve Powers—a way our innate Christ nature is able to express in our lives. On the other hand, it's a spiritual danger; Jesus constantly reminded his disciples to "Judge not." How can the same word describe both an aspect of the divine and a spiritual danger?

The difference is both subtle and important. The divine power of judgment may best be understood as "discernment." It represents our innate ability to recognize and evaluate the energy behind every choice we face. Is it an efficient use of our creative power? That is, will it provide a significant step forward on our spiritual path? Or is it an inefficient use of our power that will take us on confusing and distracting detours?

It's important to note that both options are Good, in that both are of God. It's like choosing between an eight-lane superhighway that leads directly to our next spiritual goal, or a squiggly two-lane road that takes twice as long to cover the same distance, but offers some stunning vistas and entertaining experiences along the way.

It may seem that the most efficient path is always best; but if we truly are here to create energies of love, healing and new possibilities in the world, we may well find more opportunities to do that if we get off the main road and wander awhile, meeting and interacting with others as we do.

The "judgment" that Jesus warns us to avoid, on the other hand, is inherently dualistic, and it is often directed to others as well as ourselves. It's dualistic because it retains the Satan consciousness assumption of right and wrong, with concurrent rewards or punishments. It's directed to others because it assumes we have the right to evaluate how well or poorly others are doing in terms of their relationships to the God of their beings. This understanding puts us in those empty thrones of judgment, assuming the right to decide who has—and has not—been obedient to the laws of God.

It is often assumed that this passage reflects the second, dualistic sense of judgment. People are found guilty of sins and punished accordingly. Is that really what it says? Only, I would suggest, if we approach it with that concept already fixed in our minds.

What the Revelation tells us is simply that the completion of a particular Hero's Journey requires a process of discernment, in which we recognize and evaluate the consequences we've experienced out of choices we've made.

Why? Well, so that we can learn helpful lessons that will make the next journey easier and more rewarding from beginning to end.

We've met the image of the book of life before. We are entered in the book of life once we are awake to our spiritual purpose, however vaguely we may understand it at first.

Once we set off on our first Hero's Journey—once we set foot out of that first comfort zone—we are included in the book of life. We are alive—not simply as physical beings, but as spiritual seekers, as creative expressions of the divine.

The book of life records choices and the consequences of those choices. It does so dispassionately, with spiritual discernment and without dualistic judgment. No one here is punished for imperfectly completing their spiritual assignments. Everyone in the book of life becomes part of the "second resurrection."

What about the dreaded lake of fire? It's the same here as it was when we met it earlier, in Chapter 15. It represents a sense of a return to basic spiritual energy, so that it can be reformed into new expressions.

Who goes into this lake of fire? First of all, we see the ideas of Death and Hades sent into the lake. They are lies, illusions. They have no reality in God. The very concept of Death is based on the false idea that divine life could ever be anything but eternal. Hades is based on the equally absurd idea that there could ever be a place where God is absent. They can no longer survive in our new consciousness of God as Omnipresence, Omniscience and Omnipotence. They are returned to the energy that is their substance, so that substance might be free to express in other ways.

And then "anyone whose name was not found written in the book of life was thrown into the lake of fire." If you made it through an entire human experience without ever awakening to your true spiritual identity and spiritual purpose, you didn't make it into the book of life. You'll need to try again. The lake of fire will remove the dross of one life experience, so your innate spiritual energy is free to create another opportunity.

Thoughts on Step 20: Discerning Consequences

It's impossible to overstate the extent to which a belief in Judgment Day and the vividly described horrors of hell were fixed in my impressionable mind from a very early age. They never made much sense to my intuitive mind; I remember wondering at a very early age how God could ever keep track of it all, or why He'd bother. For the nuns responsible for my religious schooling, however, sin, retribution and eternal punishment were the only important reality, and they didn't try to whitewash any of it. Quite the contrary, they seemed to secretly enjoy making us uncomfortably aware of the doom awaiting us if we died with sin on our souls. (One mortal sin would condemn us to eternal hellfire; I forget how many venial sins it took. Of course, I wasn't much of a venial sin kind of guy.) We were assured that death would come upon us when we least expected it—so the pressure was quite intense.

It's easy to laugh about now, but life lived in a shadowy consciousness of shame, fear and guilt is no laughing matter—especially if you're a child trying to find a sense of self and purpose in a bewildering world. We need to understand God as a constant source of love and guidance; we need to know that we can relax in the absolute certainty that we can never be separated from that spiritual Source. Secure in the sense of our Oneness with the divine, we would then be free to understand the process of choice and consequence required of us as we accomplish our spiritual purpose. We are instead taught that God is greatly to be feared, and we are always falling short of His expectations, earning divine anger and eternal punishment on a pretty much daily basis.

In an 1895 article in *Unity Magazine®*, Unity co-founder Charles Fillmore emphatically addressed a question about Unity's understanding of universal spiritual Truth. The correspondent wrote—in words equally as resonant today, nearly 120 years later—"I don't understand how you can deny that there is sin and evil, when you see it all about you day and night."

"You mistake our teaching," Fillmore firmly replied, "if you think we deny that there is seeming evil. What we do deny is that evil has Principle back of it. It does not come from God—man creates it, hence it is not permanent and has no power except what we give it."

He then goes on to make a very important point about just how it is that we give power to evil. "We give it this power," he writes, "in two ways: first, by doing evil and second, by fearing evil. Many refrain from doing evil, but they talk about it as a reality."

What an absolutely true, and utterly revolutionary, realization this is! Traditional views of sin and punishment, of a Judgment Day to be greatly feared, empower evil by fearing it. They assume a God that sees the same duality we do, and that dangerous assumption infinitely magnifies our own tendency to judge and punish others.

If this revelatory Hero's Journey were to accomplish nothing but to free us from this self-perpetuating delusion, it would be worth every challenge we encountered along the way. But there's more—much more—to come.

MEDITATION

I AM a whole and perfect child of God. I trust God's presence in my life as infinite love and creative empowerment. There is nothing to fear as I move forward, creating the kingdom of heaven with every loving choice.

Questions for Discussion

1. Why do you think Satan is locked up for 1,000 years? Why is it necessary to release him?
2. How is God present in the lake of fire? What is the potential Good that exists in that experience?
3. Since you are engaged in learning about this Revelation, your name is surely entered in the book of life. Can you think of a time in your life when it might not have been? What has changed in you between then and now?
4. To what extent was a fear of evil a formative factor in your childhood? How would our collective consciousness change if we truly grasped that we create the experience of evil not only by embracing it, but by fearing it?
5. If giving in to evil and fearing evil are both equally counter-productive, what should our attitude be? Why?

Step 21

CLAIMING THE KINGDOM

A m I going to sound like the most pathetic kind of Bible dweeb if I confess that I have never, ever read this chapter without choking up? Probably, but so be it. In its loving understanding of what we've been through to get to this point, and its thrilling promise of the Good we have gained as a result of our journey, this chapter offers the most profound reassurance we've received since we left the Garden, all those many roles and adventures ago. It is incomparable in its inherent beauty and vivid imagery.

Every time I read it, I am left to wonder why these wonderful images aren't the best-known part of the Revelation to John, instead of the dark and negative descriptions of our journey through the shadows. Are we really so enamored with duality that we find dragons and other threatening beasts more appealing than love and abundance? If so, can we truly wonder why our lives seem to be filled with more beasts than love?

Let's allow Chapter 21 to heal our wounds, expand our appreciation and offer us just a glimpse of how powerful and beloved we truly are. It's the one chapter that really speaks for itself; there's no need for interpretation or speculation about hidden meanings. Not that this will discourage me from making a few points along the way.

> "Then I saw a new heaven and a new earth; for the first heaven and the first earth had passed away, and the sea was no more. And I saw the holy city, the new

> Jerusalem, coming down out of heaven from God, pre-
> pared as a bride adorned for her husband."
>
> —Rev. 21:1-2

Here, in two simple statements, we have the achievement of our spiritual purpose—the reason why this Hero's Journey has been so much more important than we ever fully understood. It's important to realize that collective consciousness of the time the Revelation was written saw the earth as flat, and the sky as a bowl—or "firmament," to use the term from Genesis 1—over it. It was believed that beyond the firmament could be found the perfect expression of everything imperfectly expressed on Earth.

This may seem rather juvenile to our sophisticated scientific brains; but it's not so far removed from Plato's understanding that every tangible thing on Earth has an ideal expression in the realm of ideas, so that if every chair, for example, were to disappear from the planet, we would still have the idea—the ideal of "chair"—in consciousness and could easily make a new tangible chair. For that matter, it's not so far removed from our own understanding of mind as the creative source of everything we experience in the physical world.

The kingdom of heaven we've been striving for—however unknowingly—is here defined as the process of replacing every imperfect expression with its perfect counterpart. The perfect city of Jerusalem comes down from beyond the sky to replace the imperfect city here on earth. In fact, everything is now made perfect as the divine ideals and their physical expressions are married—united as one loving life experience.

> "And I heard a loud voice from the throne saying, 'See, the home of God is among mortals. He will dwell with them as their God; they will be his peoples, and God himself will be with them; he will wipe

every tear from their eyes. Death will be no more;
mourning and crying and pain will be no more,
for the first things have passed away.'

And the one who was seated on the throne said, 'See, I
am making all things new.' Also he said, 'Write this, for
these words are trustworthy and true.'"

—Rev. 21:3-5

This is where I start misting up, without fail. This great
promise is totally without qualification; there is no suggestion
that it is tentative or conditional. In fact, we are assured that the
promise is "trustworthy and true." We can take it to the bank!

What's most important to notice, I think—and most astonishing in terms of what we've been conditioned to believe—is
both timing and directionality. We are not carried off to a better
place somewhere else, where God is more present than he is
here on Earth. We don't go to God; God comes to us.

Well, that's not really true either, because God has never been
absent. We *believed* we were living apart from God, and now we
have come to know the truth. Our awareness of the divinity that
is everywhere present and our willingness to marry that divine
Source with our human experiences are what bring the kingdom into expression.

There is no suggestion anywhere that this experience of the
kingdom is something that can only come after death. Certainly,
if we insist on that belief, we can make that our experience. But,
as Jesus never tired of pointing out, the possibility of the kingdom is here now. It is within us. It is at hand.

I especially love the divine assurance, "See, I am making all
things new." I had a major "Aha!" moment a number of years
ago when it occurred to me, while meditating on this passage, that there is an important difference between "making
all things new" and "making all new things." I was spending
too much time waiting for the kingdom to appear as something

completely different from my present experience—a new job, a new relationship, some new money. (Actually, I would have accepted old money as well.)

But that's not the promise, is it? The promise is that the presence of God will make all things new. The elements of my life may stay the same, but I will experience them differently. I will see the divine wherever I look, for that's the nature of the kingdom.

> "Then he said to me, 'It is done! I am the Alpha and the Omega, the beginning and the end. To the thirsty I will give water as a gift from the spring of the water of life. Those who conquer will inherit these things, and I will be their God and they will be my children.'"
>
> —Rev. 21:6-7

"The water of life" is a constantly repeated image throughout the teachings of Jesus and related texts. It suggests, I think, that we might want to pay more attention to it than we have in the years since his ministry.

We've noted earlier that Jesus offers the Samaritan woman at the well "a spring of water gushing up to eternal life" (Jn. 4:14). He links this life-giving water to the I AM, the Christ Presence of divine power and understanding that lives as each of us. Here we are promised that when we are thirsty enough to ask, the water of our eternal divine nature will flow freely.

> "But as for the cowardly, the faithless, the polluted, the murderers, the fornicators, the sorcerers, the idolaters, and all liars, their place will be in the lake that burns with fire and sulfur, which is the second death."
>
> —Rev. 21:8

This is not so much a threat, or even a warning, as it is a loving description that recovery programs might label "How It

Works." Our choices must be consistent with our new kingdom consciousness in order for the eternal waters to flow freely in our lives. We cannot remain in the kingdom if we fall back into choices based on fear, greed, limitation and competition.

There is a purification process in place so the negative consequences of those fearful choices can be efficiently burned away. It may seem painful, but it's a process as steeped in love as everything is, now that our consciousness is open to the divine.

> "Then one of the seven angels who had the seven bowls full of the seven last plagues came and said to me, 'Come, I will show you the bride, the wife of the Lamb.' And in the spirit he carried me away to a great, high mountain and showed me the holy city Jerusalem coming down out of heaven from God.
>
> It has the glory of God and a radiance like a very rare jewel, like jasper, clear as crystal. It has a great, high wall with twelve gates, and at the gates twelve angels, and on the gates are inscribed the names of the twelve tribes of the Israelites; on the east three gates, on the north three gates, on the south three gates, and on the west three gates. And the wall of the city has twelve foundations, and on them are the twelve names of the twelve apostles of the Lamb."
>
> —Rev. 21:9-14

I think we've talked enough about the spiritual significance of the number 12 and its various components. To Jewish readers, the reference would be to the traditional 12 tribes of Israel. Christians would understand it in terms of the 12 apostles.

Metaphysically, there are 12 powers—12 specific energies, centered in specific physical locations in our bodies—that allow the Christ to express into our lives as the kingdom of heaven. They are faith, understanding, will, imagination, zeal, power, love, discernment, strength, order, elimination and life. The proper use of these powers is the metaphysical foundation on which the entire kingdom of heaven is to rest.

> "The angel who talked to me had a measuring rod of gold to measure the city and its gates and walls. The city lies foursquare, its length the same as its width; and he measured the city with his rod, fifteen hundred miles; its length and width and height are equal. He also measured its wall, one hundred forty-four cubits by human measurement, which the angel was using. The wall is built of jasper, while the city is pure gold, clear as glass. The foundations of the wall of the city are adorned with every jewel; the first was jasper, the second sapphire, the third agate, the fourth emerald, the fifth onyx, the sixth cornelian, the seventh chrysolite, the eighth beryl, the ninth topaz, the tenth chrysoprase, the eleventh jacinth, the twelfth amethyst. And the twelve gates are twelve pearls, each of the gates is a single pearl, and the street of the city is pure gold, transparent as glass."

—Rev. 21:15-21

As in Chapter 11, the process of measurement is a way of symbolically claiming the vision. The 12 (Again!) precious stones mentioned here correspond to the 12 stones the High Priest wears on his breastplate (as described in Exodus 28), representing the Twelve Tribes. Pearls the size of city gates and gold that is both pure and transparent suggest that the kingdom of heaven will not be limited to the realm of human possibility.

> "I saw no temple in the city, for its temple is the Lord God the Almighty and the Lamb. And the city has no need of sun or moon to shine on it, for the glory of God is its light, and its lamp is the Lamb. The nations will walk by its light, and the kings of the earth will bring

their glory into it. Its gates will never be shut by day—
and there will be no night there. People will bring into
it the glory and the honor of the nations. But nothing
unclean will enter it, nor anyone who practices abomination or falsehood, but only those who are written in
the Lamb's book of life."

—Rev. 21:22-27

Well, here's a passage you won't find preached in many
churches! There is no temple! Now that we both understand
and demonstrate the truth that we are spiritual beings eternally
one with our Source, there is no need for a hierarchical structure linking us to God. This is why it's often said that the true
purpose of a Unity minister is to put himself or herself out of a
job by empowering everyone to know and express their own
unique aspect of the divine energy we share. So there's no job
security here. However, I'm not too concerned that the empowerment will be completed any time soon. If it is, I'll be too busy
relishing the kingdom to worry about some old-consciousness
thing like a job.

Further, all apparent sources of light—sun, moon, lamps—
will also disappear, as "the glory of God" becomes our constant
light Source, and "there will be no night." Metaphysically, of
course, each of us is the city, and each of us will be centered and
radiant in our Oneness with the divine. We're again reminded
that we must continue to be "written in the Lamb's book of
life," free of unclean and fear-based choices, if we wish to stay
in kingdom consciousness.

Thoughts on Step 21: Claiming the Kingdom

Try as I might, I cannot understand how those people who
are most eager to "believe" the Revelation to John as a promise
of judgment and punishment are the same people who insist
that heaven and hell are places we are assigned after death, as a

reward or punishment for the life we've led. Such a belief gives substance and harsh reality to the concept of "death," which is precisely what Jesus Christ tried to disprove with his own crucifixion experience.

The message of the Revelation could not be clearer than it is in this chapter. The new consciousness that Jesus describes as "the kingdom of heaven" does not lie in some distant dimension, or at some future time. It will express in our lives when we make that choice—when we allow ourselves to be the channels through which God, as divine creative energy, flows into this world to transform it.

The fact that we are not experiencing the kingdom of heaven today is not because it is being withheld. God is not punishing us by withholding our good. We are punishing ourselves by refusing to believe the basic truth that Jesus taught: We are truly divine, endowed with all the qualities we define as God, and we alone have the power to create the kingdom.

I sometimes, in meditation, imagine Jesus Christ regarding us from whatever elevated dimension of consciousness he now inhabits, listening to ministers and teachers affirm—in his name!—ideas of a punishing God, a distant place called heaven, a real and fearful negative power in deliberate opposition to God. I hear him say, with a sense of bemused wonder, "Where do they get this stuff?"

The real irony is that those people who most enthusiastically embrace the Revelation to John are precisely the people who are the farthest removed from the core universal principle that the Revelation illustrates: Our nature is innately divine; there is no separation; there is no future time or dimension in which heaven may be offered to us.

The kingdom will express in whatever "now moment" we choose to believe in it, believe in ourselves and make the creative choice to bring it into being.

I sometimes wonder what might have happened to the religion of Christianity if, instead of choosing the crucifixion as its central focus, it had chosen instead an image of Peter walking on the water. Sure, he ultimately gave way to his human fears and sank; but for a while there he walked on the water! He did it! Although no one recorded the details, I suspect on many other occasions, late at night and all alone, Peter snuck down to the lake to try it again—and was able to resist the weight of fear for longer and longer periods of time.

That's all Jesus Christ asks of us—that we believe we can, and keep at it until we do. Perhaps another appropriate symbol might be the spring of living water; it's not doled out sparingly to those who can afford it or who have qualified to receive it. It exists in free-flowing abundance, available to everyone who chooses to drink—and to everyone willing to walk upon the waters of the spring to carry its kingdom consciousness to the entire world.

MEDITATION

Today my world is transformed. Today I see the kingdom of heaven, as a light of infinite love, wherever I look. In the joys and rewards of the day, as well as in its shadows and challenges, I know that I AM the creative divine Presence that is bringing the kingdom into full expression.

Questions for Discussion

1. What do you think is the difference between the old heaven and Earth and the new? How will we know when the transition has happened?

2. Some believe "Death will be no more; mourning and crying and pain will be no more" means the kingdom of heaven will be free of all challenges. Others believe the challenges will (or may) remain, but our understanding of them will change. What do you think this means?

3. Look at the eight precise "sins" that are to be committed to the lake of fire (verse eight). Can you see a common denominator among them?

4. Since there is no temple, people apparently no longer come together to worship God. Why not? Can you think of spiritual reasons they *would* come together?

Step 22

CONTINUING FORWARD

Well, I wasn't always sure we'd make it, but here we are—the final step, with nothing to do but appreciate one more time the vision at which we've arrived, and tie up a few loose ends. Can there be any question, in the sublime energy of these final passages, that the journey was well worth it?

> "Then the angel showed me the river of the water of life, bright as crystal, flowing from the throne of God and of the Lamb through the middle of the street of the city. On either side of the river is the tree of life with its twelve kinds of fruit, producing its fruit each month; and the leaves of the tree are for the healing of the nations. Nothing accursed will be found there any more. But the throne of God and of the Lamb will be in it, and his servants will worship him; they will see his face, and his name will be on their foreheads. And there will be no more night; they need no light of lamp or sun, for the Lord God will be their light, and they will reign forever and ever."
>
> —Rev. 22:1-5

This is another vivid description of how life is to be in the new consciousness that is the kingdom of heaven. It is also an intriguing demonstration of the divine guidance that so effectively combined dozens of assorted writings into the cohesive message of the Bible.

We first hear of the tree of life in the earliest pages of Hebrew Scripture, at Genesis 3:22. At that point, as Adam and Eve are leaving the Garden of Eden, the Lord stations cherubim with flaming swords to prevent them from having access to the tree. Why? Because "the man has become like one of us, knowing good and evil; and now he might reach out his hand and take from the tree of life, and eat, and live forever."

Hmmm. Apparently the fruit of the tree of life endows an awareness of the spiritual truth of eternal life, just as the fruit of the tree of the knowledge of good and evil endows an awareness of the illusion of duality.

Traditionally, it is assumed the Lord is extending his punishment of Adam and Eve for their disobedience. I think that now, from the perspective of the Bible's final chapter, we can come to a different understanding.

I think we have been kept from the tree of life as a form of loving protection. If we ate of its fruit at an earlier stage of our journey, we would live forever *at the level of consciousness we had achieved by then*. If we were still in Victim consciousness, we would forever be enacting the role of Victim. If we stumbled on the tree of life in Warrior mode, we would forever be the Warrior. We are kept from the tree for our own protection.

We are now fully the Christ. We have mastered the illusion of duality through persevering on our Hero's Journey. We have remembered and reclaimed our true spiritual identity. We can now be trusted with access to the tree of life, and here it is. It offers us 12 kinds of fruit (another reference to the tribes, the apostles and the powers), and "the leaves of the tree are for the healing of the nations."

Keep in mind the author of the Revelation to John had no idea his work would end up in something called "The Bible," much less that it would be the final work included. He could not consciously have intended to use the tree of life as a kind of closing bookend to the reference in Genesis. Yet the symmetry is clear and powerful—and, I would suggest, divinely guided.

The other important point here is the Presence of the divine as a constant, both collectively and individually. The divine name on our foreheads suggests that our minds—the repository of the mixed bag of positive and negative beliefs that have battled within us throughout our journey—will now express the Oneness that is the universal spiritual truth. It will offer a constant source of light—not that there will no longer be shadows, but that we will see the Presence of God in both shadow and light.

> "And he said to me, 'These words are trustworthy and true, for the Lord, the God of the spirits of the prophets, has sent his angel to show his servants what must soon take place.'
>
> 'See, I am coming soon! Blessed is the one who keeps the words of the prophecy of this book.'
>
> I, John, am the one who heard and saw these things. And when I heard and saw them, I fell down to worship at the feet of the angel who showed them to me; but he said to me, 'You must not do that! I am a fellow servant with you and your comrades the prophets, and with those who keep the words of this book. Worship God!'"
>
> —Rev. 22:6-9

The author again gives way to the human tendency to worship the messenger instead of receiving the message. The angel sounds fairly urgent in warning him not to do that; it seems to emphasize the danger of this last temptation—to associate the power of the message with the apparent source, instead of steadfastly worshipping its true Source, the Divine Mind of God.

> "And he said to me, 'Do not seal up the words of the prophecy of this book, for the time is near. Let the evil-doer still do evil, and the filthy still be filthy, and the righteous still do right, and the holy still be holy.'
>
> 'See, I am coming soon; my reward is with me, to repay according to everyone's work. I am the Alpha and the Omega, the first and the last, the beginning and the end.'"
>
> —Rev. 22:10-13

The prophets of Hebrew Scripture, who experienced similar visions, were consistently told to keep them secret; the world was not yet ready to know the truth. Just the opposite is true here: The vision is needed at once, because "the time is near."

This statement has often been interpreted to indicate that "the end of the world" is at hand. But these final chapters have nothing to do with the end of the world; they describe the birth of the new kingdom. As Jesus emphasized, the kingdom is always near. It is within us and among us, awaiting only our spiritual readiness and willingness to bring it into expression.

> "Blessed are those who wash their robes, so that they will have the right to the tree of life and may enter the city by the gates. Outside are the dogs and sorcer-ers and fornicators and murderers and idolaters, and everyone who loves and practices falsehood."
>
> —Rev. 22:14-15

It was in Chapter 7 that we first encountered the multitude who had (paradoxically) washed their robes white in the blood of the Lamb (Rev. 7:14). We are now one with that multitude, cleansed not by a sacrifice of blood, but by the life energy of blood—the vitality of the Christ within us.

"It is I, Jesus, who sent my angel to you with this testimony for the churches. I am the root and the descendant of David, the bright morning star." The Spirit and the bride say, 'Come.' And let everyone who hears say, 'Come.' And let everyone who is thirsty come. Let anyone who wishes take the water of life as a gift."

—Rev. 22:16-17

I am reminded in this final chapter of the passage in Genesis (Chapter 18) in which Abraham greets three travelers who turn out to be angels on their way to determine if Sodom and Gomorrah are deserving of destruction. Except that somehow, in the course of the story, the three angels become the Lord Himself, bartering with Abraham over how many good people it will take to save the two cities from ruin. Similarly here, the voice of the angel seems to intermingle with the voice of Jesus, speaking as the Christ Presence he came to express and embody.

To assume it is uniquely Jesus Christ who is "coming soon" is another cop-out. If that were the case, our job would be to simply behave ourselves and wait. This is appealing for those reluctant to claim their own spiritual obligations, but it contradicts every element of Jesus' own message and ministry. He doesn't call us to "believe" in what he did or in who he is. He calls us to discover who *we* are and to express our own Christ energy as he did his—to heal, love, feed and prosper each other as we come together to create the kingdom.

So the much-discussed, long-awaited "Second Coming" does not really involve Jesus Christ at all. His work is done. It's our turn. The Second Coming will occur when we have surrendered our collective consciousness to the Christ—the truth of our creative power. The invitation could not be clearer or more lovingly extended: Come! The waters of eternal life are waiting. The choice is ours.

> "I warn everyone who hears the words of the proph-
> ecy of this book: if anyone adds to them, God will add
> to that person the plagues described in this book; if
> anyone takes away from the words of the book of this
> prophecy, God will take away that person's share in the
> tree of life and in the holy city, which are described in
> this book."
>
> —Rev. 22:18-19

This is sort of a primitive version of a copyright page. If the vision is true—and we have been assured that it is—then it is an expression of universal truth. For us to add or subtract anything would simply represent the efforts of our mortal minds to make its message more acceptable. Those efforts would stem from deep-rooted fear of the words; that fear would increase the negative energies the words describe and would block us from the spiritual promises.

> "The one who testifies to these things says, 'Surely I am
> coming soon.'
>
> Amen. Come, Lord Jesus!
>
> The grace of the Lord Jesus be with all the saints. Amen."
>
> —Rev. 22:20-21

"The one who testifies" has presented in many forms throughout the Revelation to John—messenger, angel, Lord, Jesus, Lamb. The one identity common to every form is the Christ, the Presence and Power of the divine that is the truth of who we all are.

"Lord Jesus" will come to greet us when we have elevated our own self-awareness to the point he has reached—the point of fully expressing our identity as the Christ and our spiritual purpose of creating the kingdom of heaven.

MEDITATION

I AM peaceful and serene as I rest in the joy of a creative cycle completed through me. And I AM eager and confident as I feel the first stirrings of another cycle calling me forward. I AM comfortable now with my true spiritual nature, and with my innate ability to fulfill my spiritual purpose. I AM the Second Coming of the Christ, and I AM a co-creator of the kingdom of heaven.

Questions for Discussion

1. What is the feeling you get from the description of the "New Jerusalem" in verses 1-5? Does it seem a place of rest or activity? Is our work complete? Or is there more to do? What makes you think so?

2. What examples occur to you of a tendency to worship the messenger instead of honoring the message?

3. As you look back over your journey through this Revelation, in which part of it might you have been "washing your robe"? How does that process prepare you to enter the gate of the city now?

FINAL THOUGHTS

I said at the outset that the first seeds of this book were planted in my consciousness on the same Island of Patmos where the Revelation to John was first written. Those seeds grew out of a discontent with what seemed to me an innate conflict between the very deep and empowering energies I felt there and the very dark and negative reputation that had accrued to the Bible's final book through the centuries.

At first, that discontent led me to disregard the Revelation completely, but this began to seem inconsistent with my enthusiasm for the Bible as a whole. For such a controversial writing—even in its own time—to have such a place of honor as the final piece of Christian scripture must mean something.

So I began to dig. I found, for me, that its purpose is clear and powerful. It does not contradict the loving energy of the Gospels; it is entirely consistent with the message and ministry of Jesus Christ. It simply recognizes, and expands upon, Jesus' teaching that our individual process of moving forward through fears and distractions to a full expression of the kingdom of heaven consciousness within us is unavoidably challenging and dramatic.

I hope I have been able to communicate at least some of that loving energy in this book. You may never want to revisit the Revelation to John again, and that's fine. What's important is not that you enthusiastically embrace it in every vivid detail, but that you leave it with absolutely no fear that this final book contains negative and judgmental dictates that run counter to universal spiritual principles.

It cannot be stunning news to learn that the process of remembering our spiritual purpose, dissolving the accumulated energies of old, false beliefs and allowing the infinite creative power of the Christ to become our complete life expression is not a stroll in the park. It is a challenging journey that requires focus, fearlessness and a healthy sense of humor.

The Revelation to John helps us to understand that, no matter how much resistance we encounter, we are infinitely stronger than any of the negative energies—the beasts, the locusts, the dragons, the malignant political powers—that seem to be committed to blocking our progress.

You are a spiritual being who has come into human expression at a spiritually important time, and for a spiritually important purpose. It may well be that in the realm of spirit in which we made our commitment to this particular Hero's Journey, the negative energies we would be kicking up in the process seemed like they would be little more than mild annoyances. The power those energies have when we fully experience them may come as a shock.

If so, the Revelation to John may serve a crucial purpose as it assures us that we are always on the path, and we can never be overwhelmed.

My favorite Bible teacher, the late Rev. Frank Giudici, had an important piece of advice he was always eager to share. If you find yourself in a crucifixion experience, he said—and we experience a form of crucifixion every time we begin to move out of yet another comfort zone—it's important that you remember to stick around for the resurrection. Otherwise, you're just spinning your wheels, from one crucifixion to the next, without the payoff of spiritual elevation.

The same is true, I think, for the Revelation to John. Too many people get lost in its middle chapters, terrified by the fearful images describing the inevitable consequences of moving forward.

Please—stick around for the payoff! I try never to open the Revelation without reading Chapter 21 before I close it. That's the resurrection—the kingdom of heaven that will be created through our willingness to complete our spiritual purpose.

The destination is certainly worth the journey.

Blessings!

231

BIBLIOGRAPHY

The following works are cited or referenced in the text.

H. Emilie Cady, *Lessons in Truth*, Kansas City, Missouri; Unity Books, 1896.

Joseph Campbell, *The Hero With a Thousand Faces*, Novaro, California; New World Library, 2008.

John Dominic Crossan, *Jesus: A Revolutionary Biography*, San Francisco, California; HarperCollins, 1994.

Stevan Davies (translator), *The Gospel of Thomas*, Woodstock, Vermont; Skylight Paths Publishing, 2002.

Charles Fillmore, *The Revealing Word*, Kansas City, Missouri, Unity Books.

Barbara Marx Hubbard, *Revelation*, San Rafael, California: Foundation for Conscious Evolution, 1993.

Jean-Yves Leloup (translator), *The Gospel of Philip*, Rochester, Vermont; Inner Traditions, 2004.

Carolyn Myss, *Anatomy of the Spirit: The Seven Stages of Power and Healing*; New York, New York; Three Rivers Press, 1996.

Elaine Pagels, *Revelations*, New York, New York; Viking Penguin, 2012.

John Shelby Spong, *Re-Claiming the Bible for a Non-Religious World*, New York, New York; HarperCollins, 2011.

ABOUT THE AUTHOR

ED TOWNLEY has been a licensed and ordained Unity minister for more than 20 years, after an earlier career as an actor, director and playwright. He has served congregations in Beaverton, Oregon; Chicago, Illinois; Dallas, Texas; and Hartford, Connecticut.

Rev. Ed, as he is often called, is the author of *Meditations on the Mount*, a metaphysical appreciation of the Sermon on the Mount that was later released in paperback as *The Secret According to Jesus*. He is the host of *Bible Alive!*, a weekly program of Bible discussion on Unity Online Radio (*www.unityonlineradio.org*), and responds to requests for Bible interpretation directed to Unity's website, *www.unity.org*. Rev. Ed lives in Manchester, Connecticut, with his partner in ministry, a Welsh corgi named Bentley.

B0115

chaKras
1. coccyx - base of the spine
as a sacrement, it is
baptism

Who we are individually
within the group, survival
____ instinct
3. in the solar plexus
confirmation
white stone
4. heart - Love

5. Base of the tongue -
throat and thyroid
Personal power

6. Pineal gland
between the eyes.
third eye